T0115159

# THE POWER AND ART OF LIVING

## Teddy Smith

*Foreword by*
*Jay Gilbert, Ph.D.*
*Empire State College*
*State University of New York*

*Edited by Andrew F. Ackers*

*Photography by Gregory Price*

iUniverse, Inc.
Bloomington

# The Power and Art of Living

*iUniverse books may be ordered through booksellers or by contacting:*

*iUniverse*
*1663 Liberty Drive*
*Bloomington, IN 47403*
*www.iuniverse.com*
*1-800-Authors (1-800-288-4677)*

*ISBN: 978-1-4502-5615-5 (sc)*
*ISBN: 978-1-4502-5616-2 (ebook)*
*ISBN: 978-1-4502-5617-9 (dj)*

*Library of Congress Control Number: 2010916058*

*Printed in the United States of America*

*iUniverse rev. date: 3/16/2011*

To my mother and father
Lillian and Melvin Smith

# Acknowledgements

I would like to thank my mother and my late father for their love, support and understanding. I would also like to express my deep appreciation to a great editor and friend, Andrew Ackers, for the time, generous effort and support extended to me, along with his wonderful sense of humor. And, to Gregory Price for his own extraordinary efforts and magnificent photography. Much appreciation is extended to Professor Jay Gilbert of Empire State College, the State University of New York, for the special privilege of having him write the Foreword to the book. I would also like to thank all the very wonderful people at iUniverse who through these years have contributed significantly to the editing, production and marketing of the book, especially Brian Hallbauer and Shawn Waggener.

Recognition goes to the people interviewed for publication: Joe Franklin, "Cousin Brucie" Bruce Morrow, Gregory Prince, Virginia Olney, Dr. Stephen Scheidt, Phil Tisi, and Robert Cavaluzzi, Jr. A very personal thank you is extended to the United Nations, and especially Mrs. Sylvia Howard Fuhrman, Assistant Secretary-General and Special Representative of the Secretary General for UNIS. The following staff members have also played a major role in my success at the United Nations After-school Program: Thomas Baker, Obaya James Moore and Bridget Roberts. Additionally, I would like to acknowledge the past and present support of individuals from the broadcast industry including: Dan Ingram, Frank Truatt, WGHT Radio, and Dave Kreiswirth.

In the world of martial arts and fitness the following have directly or indirectly inspired this and many other of my own endeavors:

Sensei Richard Kim, Sensei Peter Urban, Sensei Don Buck, Sensei John Denora, Sensei Katsuo Watanabe, Sensei Don Warrener, Sensei Aaron Banks, Sensei Richard Wolicki, Sensei Jerry Thomson, Sensei Alexander Kirk, Kaicho Tadashi Nakamura, Soshu Shigeru Oyama, Sensei Goshin Yammamoto, and Master Wilfredo Roldan. And, thank you to the many teachers at the Mas Oyama School of Karate in 1974, including Master Danny Tiger Schulmann, Sensei Steve Young, Sensei Mike Spanakos, Sensei Joe Ardouin, Sensei Harry Kuhn, Sensei John Banahan, and Sensei Tony.

Throughout my educational career, the following individuals have played a significant role: Paul Paparella, Jeffrey Fisher, William Woodward, Doug Austin, Fred Weaver, Lloyd Hogan, Doug Davidson, Edward Cogan and Pavle Batanic.

Finally, I would like to thank the other friends and relatives whose personal support for many years have meant so much to my own development: Stanley Wolfe, Amanda Wolfe, Zelda Katz, Sidney Weinstein, all cousins Gerry Greenberg, Nick Ragusa, Patrick Fortune, Brad Willinger, Michael Thebner, Dave Smith, Liborio Derario, Bill Barschow, Richard Chila, Jeffrey Arnold, Alfonso Renna, Mel Klein, Bobby O'Brien, Dr. Stewart Schwartz, Dr. Syed Abdullah, Dan Romer, David Letters, Ray C., Ed Herter, Linda and Craig Harrington, Jeanne Frey, Lynn Porras Kirsh, Dr. Shephard VanGelder, Joan Berman, Ralphie Bracco, David Williams, John Luke, Mike Ellenbogen, and the Suffern High School Graduating Class of 1978. A special thank you goes to Jose for the decaf coffee and the many extra hours of writing on-premises.

# Foreword

I first met Ted Smith in the early 1990s, when he came into my office to talk with me about a series of undergraduate studies in which he was interested. At that time he had attained at least two academic degrees, having successfully completed both undergraduate and graduate study at other universities, and was a certified teacher. His request to me was not totally unusual; I am a faculty mentor at Empire State College, the alternative adult college of State University of New York, where the average student is a working adult close to 40 years old, where study documented by written learning contracts is carried out primarily independently and classroom attendance is not required, and where students with faculty support can develop their own degree program plans that can include and be based upon knowledge that they have gained through work and life experience.

At the time, Ted had been teaching physical education for many years in a New York City High School, although his teacher certification was in another area. It was for this reason that he wanted to work with me to construct a second Bachelors degree, one that would be based upon and would recognize the knowledge that he had gained from teaching physical education to middle-school and high-school age children. He talked with me in a number of our meetings over several years about his approach to teaching. It was clear from our discussions that he was bringing to his involvement with children a much broader base of knowledge and philosophy than one would normally expect to see in comparable situations.

Ted completed his degree with the college. His major was based on substantial advanced standing, granted through evaluation of his demonstrable knowledge and understanding of a wide range of areas relevant to the philosophy and practice of physical education. He wished to study and therefore included in his program several additional advanced topics in physical education, which he carried out through structured independent study, working them into his already crowded schedule and life. He demonstrated very clearly in his work with our college that he could self-start, develop study plans and goals on his own, carry out study at a high level of proficiency and performance, and successfully complete involved assignments within scheduled times. Ted is a sophisticated adult independent learner.

As you will see, these abilities were not given to Ted in the cradle but grew and evolved and matured through a thoughtful and purposeful developed path, a path that Ted develops for us and helps us reflect upon in this book. It becomes clear as you read where Ted has derived the base from which his life and life activities originate. The set of values he so simply but lovingly describes can support a strong and achievable trail not only to good learning practice, but also to learning how to share new knowledge and understanding with others in the society within which we all live. What Ted asks of us is to question our values, to consider how we might set as a goal the achievement of wisdom and an improved quality of life, and to engage the mind, the body, and the soul in an extended and exciting pathway to a better life. Read this book, take his lessons to heart, and enjoy!

Jay Gilbert, Ph.D.
Empire State College
State University of New York

# Introduction

Many of the significant answers to life's purpose do not always arrive at the same time. And, they can never be learned right away. It takes a great deal of patience, drive and persistence as well as sometimes just letting go.

More importantly, life is a challenge and a test of an individual's character, strength and humility. The many disciplines, good points of reference and virtues that we learn along the way can always be built upon and used for the benefit of others.

To help clarify the growth process developed in this book I have first referred to notes from earlier years during my educational life which closely mirror practices and activities in the present. This mirroring can not only serve as a place of reference for many other individual lives but also for those who live around us.

Secondly, with an extensive background in the martial arts, I have already developed several karate manuals and studied under some of the most important proponents of its various schools. These concentrated activities have helped to inspire many of the physical fitness routines and martial arts disciplines that I teach and strongly believe are necessary to develop the mind, body and spirit connection.

Thirdly, and pivotal to the learning process again as inspired in my current programs, is having taught at all levels of education in diversified settings. This especially includes the United Nations After-school Program and in my martial arts and fitness schools.

Teaching children, young adults and adults from multicultural and multiethnic backgrounds has enabled me to experience a wonderful sense of 'universal' context. This diversity of context and deployment of alternative education is energetically celebrated and enthusiastically accepted in all my daily teaching exercises as well as life practice.

Finally, and especially during the past handful of years, I have contemplated very much completing a book that would integrate the greater virtues: the higher qualities of life that have been taught to and by me that help develop character, improve stamina and elevate our existence to a spiritual plateau.

Many traditions speak of 'enlightenment' as a state of being, or a word incorporating a sense of openness with wisdom. However, enlightenment also requires the capacity of self-reflection, one of the core skills that all education seeks to develop in individuals. Without the capacity to reflect upon one's self in differing and objective context true judgment with respect to actions, values, morals, and even simple survival cannot be accomplished. All good judgment and actions must have proper foundation within the individual.

Since everything affects our daily lives, I slowly developed perspectives from daily life that can sustain a good, positive and improvement-oriented outlook when re-incorporated into routines. Suddenly, I was interviewing educators, practitioners and authors on my radio talk shows who were not only supportive of my thoughts and ideas but sustaining in relation to their own very educated and enlightened ideals.

You never know how one experience will lead to another. One idea can connect with another just like new friends or acquaintances can teach you in the present as well as influence your future. You don't have a definite answer as to why they are there, how they really arrived and what the connections are until you find yourself inspired or accomplished in worlds you might once have never thought possible alone.

This is why I have brought a handful of 'friends' along this journey. These friends, teachers and notables were interviewed by me to help facilitate proper passage in life, benefiting everyday living and practice. Through the inspiration and sometimes revelations each has had to impart, there is an added objectivity in the learning process as we develop together and often through the eyes of others.

Nothing seems to me to be as uplifting or as relevant as a child or adult engaged in the act of learning or teaching. Or, an individual recognized for these same accomplishments or philanthropic endeavors. So, there has been included original photography of the children at the United Nations After-school Program where I have taught. The children and adults that I have come in contact with through these particular experiences have not only significantly affected my own development but have also influenced the lives of so many others in positive ways.

I have included very specific interviews held with other individuals from different walks of life to both demonstrate as well as illustrate complementary ideas, insights and perspectives. A primary focus of the book is to better understand and consequentially assist others, directly or indirectly, in their own patterns and paths of growth and maturity. Challenging another to grasp directives, perceptions or even analogies from others is in itself an exercise in the maturing process.

Writing in a memoir fashion with consistent reference to another's very special life journey is much more than just a narrative in relative beginnings in my own on life. It is an effort to impart the benefit of one's life experiences in a way that can truly pave paths to simplify and assist progressive journeys for others. To me, an individual can never fully accomplish true physical fitness, mental fitness or spiritual development without assistance, both from within and from without. This assistance can come from a few or many other sources depending upon another's needs or inclinations. However, understanding the lives of others in historical as well as contemporary context is a very wonderful way to appreciate the wisdom from beyond that surrounds each and every one of us in very particular ways.

What can an individual gain from all of this? One can learn to be open and to live life fully and correctly for the moment, in the present and in reality. Many events in our own as well as other lives can't be fully explained but they can still happen for a reason. If you are able to become self-reflective while remaining open-minded, you can from benefit from others as well as better learn from what life itself has to offer. Together we can aspire to and create a path of enlightenment within and without that fortifies life's presence and purpose as well as further enables us all to reach that same infinite and unimaginable future.

# Chapter One

Looking into a mirror one can recognize the simplicity in the image of a life. Although life isn't always that simple, it can be. Think about your own life for just a moment. Reflect on a number of significant points that helped determine your life's course. Who were the people involved at the time? Often it is the people not just the situations that make life's course complete.

Let's ask a few questions first. Who and where are you today? Who are the people in your life that are most meaningful to you? Why are they meaningful to you?

What about the people who are no longer meaningful to you but have had positive or negative significance. Have you learned something from them? If so, what might you have learned?

Although events shape most of our lives, it is really us and others who are responsible for those events. This may seem fairly obvious, but you would be amazed how often this simple fact is overlooked. Many of us become overwhelmed by situations, forgetting that they are only the direct or indirect result of our own actions or the influence of others. Therefore, our own perceptions or impressions of ourselves and others can significantly change the meaning and outcome of events.

Take a deep breath for a moment. Slowly exhale. Try to get closer to your unconscious mind and better understand what you see or feel.

Now, close your eyes. After counting to twenty, slowly open them. What did you see? What did you experience? What did you feel? Where did you feel it? Are you alert or are you tired? Are you focused or unfocused? Are you satisfied? How we feel is often the result of a few seconds interlude between our conscious and subconscious minds. Yet, each level of unconsciousness as well as consciousness brings with it a myriad of alternatives if only we would choose to seek them. And, it takes just a moment to alter one's thought process. This means that it should only take a few moments to change how we feel at any given point in time in a positive way.

All the alternatives are there waiting to be explored. Happiness, peace, tranquility, and joy are attainable realities. Yet often we feel trapped or just part of a series of situations that we'd like to escape. We are too often confined sometimes for hours, days, weeks, or even years by our feelings. These feelings can create negative circumstances around us.

Now, let's ask ourselves several series of questions. We can start with an environmental check at our workplace. Again, pause to answer each of the questions.

How do you feel about your work environment? Does it have a positive or negative effect on your work process? What are the people like where you work? Is your desk surrounded by other people and desks, or do you work alone or at home? Are there windows nearby or are you in an inside cubicle? Now you can begin to understand whether or not your daily surroundings significantly affect the ways in which you think, feel or react towards yourself and others.

Is your boss friendly or mean, reactive or non-reactive? Do you feel pressures from your job: stress, competition, rivalry, or jealousy from coworkers? If you find that you are content with your work situation because the physical space surrounding you is adequate and the people are supportive, then you are at least one step ahead of many others. Now, let's flip to the home environment where there are many questions to ask yourself, even if just for positive reinforcement, along with many benefits to gain. What is your favorite room like? Do you have interesting pictures on your walls? What are they pictures of? To you, what do they represent?

Is your favorite room at home spacious or small, cluttered or uncluttered? Do you have a window to look outside? If so, what do you see when you look: a park, a tree, mountains, people, or buildings?

How often do you spend time in your favorite room giving yourself quality time? Is quality time important to you? If so how and importantly, why?

What is the rest of your house or apartment like? Do you have much furniture, office or personal equipment, kitchenware, or books?

Have you cleaned out your closets lately? What did you find in them the last time you cleaned: old shoes, out of fashion clothing or papers? When was the last time that you actually looked deep into your closets? Do you have an attic? If you do, what do you keep there, quantity or quality?

Are you a neat freak or are you sloppy and collect everything like a pack rat? Do you collect jewelry, coins, baseball cards, or old quilts? Are gifts from others important to you? What is important to you and why?

These questions should be asked successively and their answers thought about, some perhaps even for a while. Many people go through life accumulating a wide variety of items that relate to life but never really contemplate the meaning behind them. We know we like clothing but we don't know exactly why. We understand we have an enormous CD collection that we enjoy but never stop to think that we re-play only a fraction of it.

We clean out our closets or climb up to the attic every once in a while but never get around to throwing anything away. Or, we make periodic clean sweeps and everything seems to go. What is there in your physical surroundings that significantly matters you or others? What could you live without?

If we take a break and then re-approach ourselves from a different objective view, we can indeed get a little deeper inside ourselves. For instance, do you feel that you are happy? Happiness comes very much from within and can influence a total outlook on life, affecting all aspects of daily living: mental, emotional, spiritual, and physical.

What about the quality of your life? Is exercise and physical fitness part of your daily regimen? How often do you work out? Do you have your own program or does someone assist? Are you fit? Not so fit? Want to be fit? Don't really care? Are you a member of a gym or health club? Do you play sports, bowl, sky dive, scuba dive, or swim?

What about mental exercise? Do you like to read books? What kind of books? Do you enjoy reading poetry? Or, do you just read the headlines of the local daily, the sports or arts section of the national weekly, or the tabloids? What benefits from reading do you feel that you are gaining that can contribute to physical, mental, emotional, and spiritual growth and development.

Maybe you prefer music to reading. Music is of great significance. They say that music moves the soul. I feel strongly that it can move mind, heart, body, and soul.

What is your favorite genre of music? Who are your favorite artists or composers? How does music affect your feelings or moods? Does it remind you of a particular period in life when that special type of music was popular?

And of course, film. Do you prefer theaters, television, DVD, or videos? Would you prefer being alone or with others when you view films?

You see, the quality of your life is influenced either positively or negatively by a number of internal as well as external factors. For instance, we all know that fitness plays an integral part of maintaining stamina as well as proper physical, emotional and mental wellbeing. This is an objective fact. But, how important a role does it play in your own life?

Similarly, where Mozart might be soothing to one individual, Enya or Madonna might be to another. If one's life is rather dull, then rock, hip-hop, classical, jazz, or pop music might be the right antidote.

Similarly, many people still enjoy reading. It is an intellectual pastime that stimulates mental response unlike any other. While reading the newspaper to become better informed is of value to one individual, re-reading a great classic or paging through a new bestseller is important to another. However, in each of these cases an individual is influencing his or her quality of life simply by acting in a positive way.

Spending quality time on constructive activities at work, alone and in family life is healthy. Spending quality time with others in mutually beneficial activities is also healthy. All are enriching experiences. The point is to increase the level of quality activity by reducing the negative people, situations and thinking in your life. Increasing quality time reduces time spent in inappropriate and often self-destructive ways.

Now, let's step back again for just a moment. What did you study in school and has it significantly influenced what you are doing today, either in your career or in your personal life? Have you kept track of your personal as well as professional development throughout the years in terms of academia, especially continuing education?

What did you like or dislike about school? What were your classmates interested in during those years? Were you a member of a group? Were you a quiet or loud kid, an extrovert or introvert? What did you get out of your school experience? Did it have a major impact on what you are doing now and if so, how?

You see, we are also the sum total of all we have been, experience but importantly, learn. Although much of who we are can stem from how or where we were brought up as children, what we have become can begin simply when we start making our own choices. In Western culture many of those choices can be fostered in and around educational environments.

Many lives are limited by lack of intellectual or vocational training. But even more lives are limited by an inability to properly relate to choices from the past: our likes and dislikes, talents and inclinations, yearnings and strengths, and especially, personal and professional relationships. Too often the underlying positive aspects in our lives, many of which began during school years, have been overlooked or are exchanged for less qualitative choices or activities in adulthood.

We often find activities that have proven beneficial in our past being supplanted through the years by less enjoyable or less beneficial alternatives. Some of our good first choices in life have also been usurped by bad. Smoking, drinking, casual sex, or other dangerous pastimes and vices can catch us unaware. Suddenly we're traveling down a road that has little or no value to our overall growth and in fact will lead to destruction in one way or another, for ourselves, others and even those that we love most.

Remember, our feelings about a given situation can change with a moment's contemplation and redirection. How often do you push the button on the TV or home entertainment remote to change the channel or mode, alternating from sports to news, history to mystery, audio to video? Well, it's just that easy with emotions. That short trip from conscious to subconscious can find us enlivening happiness, joy and patience instead of negativity because all those feelings are also right there just beneath the surface.

Let's add a little more forethought and ask a few more questions. What is your favorite movie? Do you like to go to movies often? Are comedies your first choice or dramas? Maybe high-tech movies or science fiction? What are your favorite television shows?

Or, are you're an artist? Do you prefer Michelangelo, Da Vinci, Monet, Manet, Picasso, Chagall, or Calder? Do you like to draw, paint or sculpt? What type of pleasure do you derive from art? Is it calming to you, harmonizing or do you create chaos in your art.

One individual's pastime can be another's profession. In the cases of film, TV and art, or with books and music, you may also make your living from your favorite pastime. This is one way that quality of life can simultaneously improve both personal and professional experience. If you studied your craft in school and enjoyed it then, you may have taken with you intellectual knowledge acquired throughout the years. In this particular circumstance you should have created a present with quality of life developed in very rich historical context.

Almost anyone could have evolved as a result of his or her positive activities and inclinations from youth. Many of those positive activities and inclinations can translate into both the personal and professional arenas. However, you would be amazed at how few individuals employ personal, educational or professional preferences from when they were young.

What is your family like? Do you have children? Do you have cats or dogs? How do they relate to you?

If you have children, what was the experience of seeing that first born for the first time or at the very first moment? How did it change with each subsequent time or child, or did it?

How important is respect in your family? Do you get along with your siblings? In what ways are they different from you? If you don't have siblings, what is it like to be alone?

The point here is that events are tempered by personalities. If you are happy at work and happy at play but unhappy at home, then one negative could outweigh many of the positives. People can overshadow situations with enormous import, but only if we let them.

If you are dissatisfied at work and have little downtime for other interests but have a lovely wife and three adoring children, that can seem to make up for everything. But, does it? Remember the quality of your life is really a set of moment-to-moment experiences. It can change at the drop of a dime. Quality experiences carry through into other aspects of life, sometimes consciously and sometimes subconsciously. Regrettably, so can unpleasant circumstances.

What is your state of mind right now? Why do you remember certain events that have happened in your life? Are they often good or bad events?

Let's continue to reflect. What are the most important aspects of your life? With what you already understand from contemplating these questions, how could you improve the quality of your life immediately? What would you change? What wouldn't you change? Do you think that you could find right alternatives or balance? Perhaps you think that you can over time.

Do you have a certain passion that you are just now developing? Are there certain inspirations or aspirations you might be considering today?

What are your friends like? Can you say that you have had one or two great friends in your life? Can you share secrets or actually be yourself with them?

Balance is a final frontier for achieving harmony in life. Mind, body, spirit, and soul along with their inter-relationship with the proper people, places and events in personal and professional experiences are what make up much of the sum total of our existence. It is the balance between good and bad people, experiences and even objects in our lives, and how we learn from both internal and external factors, that can determine or undermine our own life's outcome.

What do you feel the overall condition of your internal or external life is like? Do you feel an integral part of a small or larger society? Do you care one way or the other? Are you ever really conscious of your true emotions and feelings? Are you truly cognizant of your lifestyle and the circumstances that have led you to the path that you are on right now? Are you able to learn, benefit or change by better understanding experiences?

In what ways do you believe your perspectives have changed in the last several years? Has that change made a difference in the way you view people or the way that you think they see you now? Can you say that there has been one person in your life that has inspired you or enlightened you? If so, what circumstances created that influence and in what way has it affected your perspectives?

In what ways have you reconciled differences among people in your life? Do you know when it's time to move on to a new experience or new beginnings filled with new possibilities?

It is sometimes necessary to break the bonds between yourself and others to effect positive change. Detachment or realignment is not always bad. Meditation and prayer are often singular experiences that can draw us away from others in a positive way, at least for short periods of time. However, it is often the ability to change that becomes the obstacle to overcome. Complacency, lack of ambition and certainly the inability to act upon positive impulse or assume productive initiative can have frustrating and strongly detrimental results.

What do you really want from your life? Well, it's time to take action. Find the nearest mirror and look straight into it. Watch the light behind or in front as it travels to your eyes and then feel it radiate through your entire body. As you look into the mirror, what impressions, thoughts and feelings are you now experiencing?

Think of your life situation. Is there anything that you would want to change as you observe it now? Just pause for a moment. What would that something be? Okay, now step away from the mirror and turn around. Take a few deep breaths and then exhale slowly.

Remember, that ultimate quality of life is still affected by the sum total of your experiences. So, let's begin to travel. In what ways have you changed over the years?

Think very carefully about what it was like growing up as a child. We know that our childhood years were significant but that our present life has been positively or negatively influenced by choices. So, like *Alice in Wonderland*, watch yourself become smaller and then large again! Get through those first years in elementary school, the first kiss and then the first dates in junior high school. Move beyond the good teachers and the bad teachers, the friends and the enemies for just a moment. It's now only you that we're concerned about.

Reach near full height and enter high school. And, as you enter high school, don't move, but pretend that you are stepping into the looking glass. That's right. Pretend it is no longer today but yesterday. And, that you are no longer here but back in time, the day you entered high school.

Now, let's pretend that the day was some time during the 1970s. You remember the 1970s don't you? And if you don't, think of what it might have been like. It is the starting point for our journey because it is the time when the world began another big leap into the new century era.

If we are the sum total of all our life experiences, then we must somehow have been influenced by the experiences of life during the past handful of decades. In fact it is hard to escape the world of today without understanding the world of yesterday. But you've just done it!

You are now alive on the other side of the mirror and will soon experience a world unlike the one you have actually emerged from. By the time you arrive back to today you will have had the opportunity to reform that world significantly. You will have had the opportunity to make new choices, select new alternatives and re-pattern your past. Not of course by altering history, but by altering your reactions to and feelings about it. This means to re-develop the quality of your life experiences and bring those experiences into the present.

Sound like a second chance at living? Well it is, only better. By making informed proper choices as an outgrowth from your own life path, inner yearnings and sincerest ambitions, you can position new opportunities in life and effect positive change. And, change is what you can use to facilitate the rest of your life in balance and well-poised harmony for the future.

*Lillian Smith, Teddy Smith and Melvin Smith*

# Chapter Two

To travel back in time and correctly rediscover the past you also need to be able to approach the past in light of today. How have you changed? How has society changed? What might you have done differently? Who or what has made a substantive impact on your life? Have certain events, a friend, a relationship, music, a TV show, or film helped to shape the way you think? If so, how and why?

Can you look back and get to the root of some of the differences in lifestyle or problems that affect you? Some of the situations that you're not really happy with can be rediscovered and resolved. But, you should first be willing to rid yourself of any feelings of confusion or apathy with respect to your life today.

We need to see if there are ways to reshape some of the bad feelings that we may have experienced or may not even be aware are hindering improved performance and increased happiness. Is there a special way to get deep into your core, your true nature, and truly understand? We should examine trauma, excessive baggage or other deep-rooted feelings that have or can create an impasse in the developmental process.

The past really does hold the key to the present as well as the future. What events or knowledge of events during the past forty years have actually jolted you: coming out of Vietnam, JFK, Martin Luther King, 'Reaganomoics,' the turn of the millennium? In particular, the 1960s and 1970s were, in many ways, turbulent because of dramatically changing values. Those particular decades dealt with alternatives like gurus, Watergate, women's rights, gay rights, and Vietnam. Do you remember the fall of Saigon, Saturday Night Fever or Grease? How about the overthrow of the Shah of Iran?

What about the 1980s: the Iran Contra scandals, the computer and technological boom? Do you see yourself as a better person as a result of what happened externally during those decades?

How did the 1990s, the Clinton years and capitalist expansion affect you, your culture or conditioning? The fitness boom and workout gyms were also on the rise during the 1990s.

Are you a part of the good health and holistic wave?

The new millennium brings with it more information-driven technology, computerization, automation, and a much quicker-paced society. The world and society always change, but so must we as individuals. As 9/11 struck and while terrorism continues around the world, people are becoming more aware of other ways of life and approaches to resolving social, economic and political issues. There are good and bad people everywhere. The many who gave their lives to help others in that debacle, and the very many more that have subsequently rallied support, attest to a continuing balance between good and evil.

Do you have a thirst and quest for knowledge? Can right action help you within during good as well as turbulent times?

How can we as individuals become more compassionate, dedicated and focused as we go through difficult times, or even good times? What ways can love, perseverance, patience, and integrity become the cornerstones for the betterment of our lives and society? Can you adapt and really practice as well as live up to righteous words such as: character, religion, courtesy, loyalty, and respect. Can these words become actions that are developed, nurtured and bestowed upon others throughout our lifetimes?

Conversely, does greed, power, anger, arrogance, hatred, lust, or false pride eat away at your physical, emotional and mental health and wellbeing? What can we learn from humility and the goodness in ourselves and mankind? How can we attain wisdom and insight and avoid ignorance?

It becomes obvious in life that the tools with which we need to accomplish right actions are first found within not without. Faith, hope, religion, grace, correct belief systems, moral education, right reading, correct adult learning and studying can all help evoke and guide us along a proper maturing path.

The past can also hold keys to these positive concepts. No generation since our first progenitors on earth, Adam and Eve, has ever been without one version or another of these same problems and alternative solutions. In the case of this particular first family outside of the Garden of Eden there were fields to be tilled, sheep to be raised and food other than fruit to be found. No generation has been without alternatives, although many have been denied access.

Do you believe in good and evil, moral, immoral, or amoral? Do you feel good energy in certain people and bad energy in others? Are you finding the answers within? Or, do you think that they are without? There is nothing more historical than the struggle between good and evil, whether we recognize it, believe in it or understand the struggle it represents in everyday life.

Can you talk to anyone from any background without feeling insecure? There is also always a question of image. Is image important to you? Do you need approval from others? Or, can you feel passionate enough about yourself and your life?

Theologians believe that we are made in the image and likeness of God. Do you believe in God? Do you have a belief system? Does it include Moses, Jesus, Buddha, Hindi gods, angels, or heaven? Is it based on good and evil, moral or immoral? Or, is it a worldly belief system based upon human knowledge and material counterparts. If so, then whose image are you made in? Your own, your family's, a friend's, or society's?

If we are going to try to get back to basics, then these questions also need to be asked. There is nothing more basic than the source of all humankind. With a source, there is a resource. Without a source, well, there can be problems. You don't have to have answers yet. They'll come - in time.

As you look back on your life can you find some true meaning for your own existence? What about the lives of others? If you can, great. Even if you can't, let's keep traveling. This time we'll travel without so many questions, and with a friend.

# Chapter Three

As a boy growing up in the suburbs of a small town in upstate New York, life for me was fairly simple. I knew that I liked playing with boys and girls of my own age. Floor and field hockey were always fun even after getting hit with the stick in the shins, of course by mistake.

Summer camp was always fun, especially the pretty girls on the bus. Hearing them talk about boys: the way we parted our hair, which boys were cute, who laughed more, and then about all the sleepovers that were important to them.

Of course, we usually remember the important things in life. And then, things that just seemed important to us at the time. I recall memorization was not always the easiest for me early on. I couldn't read as fast as some of the other students. Not everyone learns at the same pace.

Putting in the effort is at least half the battle. Getting assistance can make up for the other half. Some people just give up, or worse, decide not to even try. Some of the most difficult tasks can actually be accomplished through self-determination, others might need assistance. First looking within and then learning to properly reach out could prove to be all we need as methods or tools to accomplish our goal and to correctly grow.

Birthday parties were often fun. I remember my friend Stephanie's birthday party. She was ten. We were listening to the Beatles, Bob Dylan and Frankie Valli. I remember singing happy birthday and her cat jumping into the cake. We were all startled and laughed.

Learning and growing can be fun processes with the good times often far outweighing the bad. And, good times can insulate and support us from surprise or unwanted events.

Did you ever have an apple tree in your backyard? If you grew up in the country like I did, you might have had magnificent apple trees and orchards. I remember climbing an apple tree. It was great exercise getting up the tree but sometimes more difficult coming down.

My friend and I enjoyed playing on the monkey bars outside school during lunch hour. It was also special to be so lucky to have a big field outside of school to play ball. We enjoyed this very much.

You seem to get over things much quicker when you're young. You are also more willing to take risks that you might not, or should not, as an adult. There is often a sense of daring and the willingness to take advantage of opportune circumstances when they present themselves. Adults often put barriers or roadblocks based upon fear or worry that inhibit their ability to take chances. A young person's mind is often less inhibited and a willingness to learn can be at the vanguard of experience. Young or old there should also always be enough time for fun.

Mostly everyone in America gets through elementary school or schooling. It moves quickly during those years. It's a time when you are supposed to learn the basics: math, the sciences, grammar, history, and reading skills. I tried my best to learn. Some subjects were easier than others but I always made the effort. And, I learned.

I remember that my art teacher used to scream so loudly that my paintbrush would drop out of my hand. Basically, my teachers at the early stages of education were firm and didn't play games. They expected a lot out of us even if they did bore us some of the time.

Pressure is greater today for our youth than it was back then. We sometimes forget as adults how truly difficult it is, not only for ourselves, but others. When that pressure spills over and into the lives of our children we know that there has to be a problem.

Many of our children's faults are really because of our own adult shortcomings. Children see, hear and act upon what they are exposed to by adults. As adults, we are all very much better informed, especially today. Adults have access to information to make them well aware of the dangers that can negatively impact children's lives.

Youth has similar access to knowledge through technology. Education further supplies information, develops communication and can open the door to many different forms of mind and body experience. However, it is human experience as it is shown, recognized and explained through right actions that can become the greatest teacher of all.

I remember that I used to make up my own dances and karate moves during gym class as sort of the warm-up exercise for class. Kids found this very interesting and I guess sometimes funny because my exercises attracted attention. As a result, they more enthusiastically took part in the lessons. These were some of our best workouts.

We had open fields in those days and lots of space to play. I also had a Schwinn bicycle. Man, it went fast. Riding hills was a real thrill. Even in the mud the bike flew!

Physical activity of any kind was as important to me then as it is today. Most people slow down as life progresses. For some reason, I sped up. It wasn't that I needed to live in the fast lane all the time. It was that I always needed to be active instead of reactive or passive.

Physical activity is a great outlet for all kinds of emerging emotions and trends for kids. It is simple and natural. For adults, it is still the simple and natural alternative to mental activity. Adults don't always choose physical activity as a functional source of positive and negative energy release. We've been conditioned into other pastime activities. Many are passive activities like television, CD's or radio. Some activities are actually regressive, like becoming a couch potato or playing one song or type of music over-and-over.

You don't realize how great it is to be a child until you're an adult. No responsibility, great fun, friends to play with. Of course, some of us have not had pleasant childhoods, and for this I am truly sorry. Hopefully we can make up for those years in a different more productive way soon.

I had my taste of first real tragedy at an early age. When I was eleven my good friend died. He was only thirteen. It was very difficult for me. We used to ride bikes together. He had his hair cut downtown and on his way home there was a sharp curve in front of my house. A car swerved right into him.

We were close friends and it hurt for a long time. He always smiled and had a good heart. That's how I'll remember him.

As we grow up, tragedy becomes more and more a part of real life. Some of us depersonalize and begin to see that unpleasant circumstances are just part of the human condition. We learn about suffering of a much greater magnitude throughout history and especially in the lives of others. We can become more willing or able to accept situations or incidents in our own lifetimes that might otherwise appear out of scope or less conducive to positive change by better understanding other people's suffering.

Regrettably, some others overreact and let difficulty sweep them up like sands on the seashore. We are much more capable than just grains of sand and much more adaptable on our own accord. Shorelines gradually erode, but we don't need to be victims of situations, natural or otherwise. Together we can conquer almost any external force. Alone, we should always stand tall in the face of adversity and attempt to effect positive change.

I had a little AM transistor radio and used to scan the stations all the time. It became my companion and sometimes even my friend. I heard some great rock 'n' roll on one of those stations and the powerful jingles blasted through the speaker. I remember one of the jingles beamed, "Cous-in Brucie!" who played the top pop hits at the time. Another rang clear, "D-an Ingram," who was also at Music Radio, WABC.

Junior high school is an excitingly 'true' experience. It's a time when your voice changes and you end up with new exuberance and energy. Today, they call it hormonal. I just knew that it meant change.

My school had many trees. The trees made it easy to hide or relax during a lunch hour. I remember one student eating a peanut butter and jelly sandwich with chocolate chip cookies between the peanut butter and jelly. Children do things that are sometimes unusual to adults. Yet, we as adults often act like children. How often do we unnecessarily consume too many chocolate chip cookies or make an unnecessary peanut butter and jelly sandwich while watching a series of favorite sitcoms or a good HBO movie.

The lines seemed blurred back then between the acceptable and unacceptable. We weren't as informed about the consequence of things like illicit drugs. In retrospect, I realize that much of this was external or sociological change. So many 'new' things were entering into the world of American youth. Sometimes there weren't precedents already set for youth or even adults to properly understand and then work through the consequences.

Today this is not at all so. We know the dangers of many of the vices that have crept into our society throughout the past several decades, and the consequences of all those that preceded them. For instance, cigarette smoking can cause lung cancer and other diseases. The use of illicit drugs will cause addiction and eventually, brain damage. It is important for us to remember what it was like when there was more innocence in our own lives and in those around us. In other words to become a child again we must re-learn how to keep it simple.

Wrestling practice in junior high school was intense. I remember Coach Ike. The heat was turned up real high so that we would make weight for the next competition. Although he was tough, the coach always smiled and had a positive attitude.

I used to work out with Big Pete. He was over six-feet-two and weighed over two hundred pounds. When he shot a take down you'd sure know it. You'd hit the floor so fast that you wouldn't know what happened.

It's so easy to stand back and exclaim, "The bigger they are, the harder they fall!" Not so in wrestling. You really have to know how to be taken down.

Do you know what it's like to fall? To be taken down over and over again? You know what, it makes you tough. You learn what it takes to get yourself back up again. Sometimes that rebound is really the best part of it all. Afterwards when you finally double flip the next guy, it feels good. Not too good, just good.

Did you ever feel that you were in a group of people but not really feeling part of the group? That was me. I loved people but never really wanted to be led or become part of a group. Junior high had its own cliques and I was able to remain on the outside, still maintaining friendships. This was important to me then and still is today.

I began taking karate and judo lessons at a nearby school. It was quite gratifying in terms of the workouts. The first thing I noticed when I walked through the door was that everyone was sitting with their eyes closed in a still position. I wondered why. Then I realized that they all looked and were relaxed and peaceful.

The instructor was involved in all the workouts, from kicking to sit-ups to punching and sparring. The fighting seemed very intense and no one was wearing protective equipment.

During the first lesson, the instructor asked us to move our right feet into a 'C' position, like a 'C' step. I tried it and then did the same with the left foot. He then asked us to cover our face with our left arm as our right arm came down to meet the left. This was called a "high block." Amazingly, these exercises not only helped improve balance but concentration skills as well. It is now proven that these types of disciplines help improve student grades.

Physical activity fosters better overall health and wellbeing. Balance is one of the final phases of quality of life, not only as it affects our own lives, but the lives of those around us. We should have a tool, or series of tools, that not only strengthen our physical wellbeing but also improve overall stability and mental capabilities. I didn't expect that outcome when I began to study karate and judo, but now I understand the peace the others were feeling with their eyes closed at the beginning of each lesson.

Back in school I remember Mr. Pap, the principal. What a motivator and genuinely nice person he was. School plays and choir were an important aspect of school. Mr. Pap had a great way of putting together excellent performances. He worked so hard and with such dedication into the late evening hours preparing for productions or other school activities.

In education today you can still find devoted educators and teachers. Both as a teacher and student I find many examples of devotion to youth and willingness to go the extra mile. You see its one thing to have ambition, work long hours and try to beat-out the next guy for personal gain. It's quite another to do the same for the sake of others. Unbalanced self-interest generates negative energy while altruism promotes a positive energy flow.

Deductive reasoning can also play a major roll in today's society and is the cornerstone for science itself as we understand it. Science is responsible for so much of everyday life: the more balanced food we eat, the houses we sleep in and the technology we use. However, every once in a while it is smart to take a step back and use the inductive rather than the deductive method of reasoning. Be open to new concepts and ideas, challenging your perception and then perspectives along the way. The greater artists and scientists of all time used both observation and information to discover and relate.

Take a few moments to think. Close your eyes and ask yourself the question, "Do I really observe?" Wait before you answer and then open your eyes again. What do you see?

I remember that there were woods near and surrounding the school where students could participate in cross-country touring and running. The trails were long and winding. Not only were the woods a physical challenge but they were also a place to stop and pause. There were so many things in the woods that were different than in the suburbs and all the cities and larger towns that surrounded us. Just to take the time to sit under a tree alone and watch the different insects and flies, the birds, different flora and fauna, was always an experience. It makes one stop and think.

It was fun to be a kid and share some of the innocent experiences that make youth a gift to the young. Also, it's not so easy to fool a child because a child is prone to circumspection and investigation.

All those youthful experiences eventually add up to adulthood. No matter how old we are when we start, growing up is a process that takes time, effort, reflection, and a true understanding of one's inner self. Understanding the lives of others can often show us patterns that we can choose or not choose to use ourselves. Once this takes place, you naturally become a leader instead of just a learner or follower. Learning to think of others and becoming a good leader becomes the next or adult phase in the growing and maturing processes.

# Bruce "Cousin Brucie" Morrow
# Radio Personality

*Bruce Morrow has been inducted into the Radio Hall of Fame, Cable and Broadcasting Hall of Fame, NAB Hall of Fame, and has been honored at the Rock and Roll Hall of Fame. Currently with Sirius Satellite Radio as an on-air personality, he was formerly with CBS FM radio 101.1, WABC Music radio 77 AM and WNBC radio 66 AM, all in New York City. He is also president of Variety, an active children's charity.*

*In the process of questioning as well as stepping through several hours with one of the handful of individuals I think exemplifies the qualities of leadership and can improve other's lives, I have found that Bruce Morrow, also known as "Cousin Brucie," indeed fulfills this ideal. As a legendary radio personality and an entertainment industry professional, he has especially transcended the more secular and selfish roles many celebrities assume, and has established himself as a leader who's fundamental goals are also dedicated to others. "I'm a very lucky guy; I love what I do," Morrow explains.*

*He answered questions about the positive attitude of leadership from the outset with such responses as, "I have a very good feeling in my belly when I go to sleep at night knowing that I'm trying my best to help people." And he continued to provide fundamentals for effective leadership applicable not only within his field but also in his personal life.*

*Bruce Morrow traces his entertainment business history back to the 1950s when he states that at that time, "It was the radio business and the music business. Today, however, we are in the business of radio. So today, we really stress the business side of broadcasting."*

*Throughout the years Bruce Morrow has become a very substantial public radio personality who has tutored and trained other radio personalities. Bruce owned and operated many radio stations and gave the benefits of his experience to his employees.*

*His particular statements not only imply a leader who is willing to persevere in spite of adversity, but also one who is ready to adapt to conditions as they unfold. His personality and positive attitudes can also provide the strength to maintain one's own leadership perspective and impetus no matter what situation unfolds. As Morrow explains, "You need to be positive and you just try to make people feel good about themselves. The nicest and most wonderful feeling in the world, the most important part of life, is probably helping each other and giving back. There is nothing more gratifying and special than when I go to a hospital and I know that I have had something to do with building a pediatric oncology ward and helped save the lives of children. Parents and children come over to me, they hug and thank me. And, I thank them for giving me the opportunity. Not only am I improving the quality of other people's lives, but also my life quality. It's like a beautiful painting."*

*Too often leaders in general assume a sense of authority and put their own thoughts, desires, aspirations ahead of the care and concern of those entrusted to them. Bruce Morrow and I both feel strongly about this.*

*When approached with the question of work ethic, Morrow explains that, "I work hard trying to keep my audience in mind and always giving my listeners the utmost respect."*

*He also explains how important youth are in public oriented businesses such as entertainment and insists that he stays young by remaining happy himself and simply enjoying what he does. If a leader really does not enjoy what he or she is doing and becomes unhappy because of personal or professional reasons, their performance will suffer and new leaders will find a way to rise to the occasion. It is as difficult for a leader to fool the public. Bruce Morrow explains, "Today's radio audience, especially, is a very sophisticated audience. You can't fool them."*

*My concern for Morrow's ability to indirectly as well as directly lead the many who have followed his shows and his life was well-addressed. "Radio is a living business and has to constantly move on." He has proven this by creating change in the musical minds of very large audiences by being among the first to play The Beatles, Rock and Roll, Motown, and Disco. Recognizing these musical styles and trends as part of a new emerging American culture makes Morrow through the arts and through the year's a well-respected leader.*

*When the radio business in more recent times became economically threatened, Bruce Morrow once again rose to the occasion and he has had the power and influence as a direct leader to take a personal and professional stand. "As long as we can maintain diversity, live radio represents a specific market."*

*Bruce Morrow feels that the negative aspects of commerciality in the radio business can be minimized. "To me, a leader who can stand in today's very commercial and often economically troublesome times and not give in to financial influences based upon self-interest is not just a leader but a very strong leader, indeed."*

*Bruce Morrow is also highly recognized for his charitable work with children. His direct support through sponsorship and physical appearance again proves his holistic as well as universal approach to leadership as a giving back to society. "Not only am I improving the quality of other people's lives, socially, physiologically and physically, but I am also improving the quality of my own life. I've always wanted the opportunity to pay back. It's very important - - a kind of allegiance to the public that you owe. This is accomplished not only by achieving positive success in one field of leadership, but extending that leadership to other areas or initiatives that can better others."*

*True leaders are not only able to lead within a given constituency, but will have a way based upon inner strength and well-being to continue to lead outside a chosen arena when they apply the qualities of good leadership to appropriate new challenges. "I've always had one theory and one ethic. I was brought up to be involved with people, not to be negative, to see if you can change the negative into a positive. I have always found throughout life that it is so much easier to be positive than to be negative. It takes to much energy to be negative. I'm trying to keep a positive attitude through the power of broadcasting, which is a wonderful medium when used properly. When used positively, you reach people and you can stimulate them into doing positive things. That's the magic of broadcasting."*

*For Bruce Morrow, that means not only withstanding the right and wrong currents of change in time, but maintaining self-identity that can be recognized. With the opportunity and ability as a broadcast personality to both directly and indirectly effect positive change in others, and the willingness to extend that outreach outside the spectrum of his general public to those who are less fortunate and in need, Bruce Morrow proves to be a universal, consummate and tireless leader. Belief, perseverance and unwavering moral ethic, as well as a willingness to give, can make a true leader not only better, but benefit others in the process.*

*Bruce Morrow*

*Teddy Smith and Bruce Morrow*

*Teddy Smith and Bruce Morrow*

# Chapter Four

In 1974 I entered high school. During my high school years I met some of the greatest kids in the world. The memories of many continue to inspire me today. I know that I have helped at least a few of them on life's journey.

The school I attended was located in the Ramapo Mountains in New York State. It's a small town area but magnificently beautiful, filled with nature and very real things.

I remember walking into the foyer of the school and being in awe of the large hallways. Deep corridors and the spacious beautiful interior design and architecture made it different. My father used to say it looked like a country club. The school facilities included a swimming pool, planetarium and beautiful hills on the property. It was also a great place conducive to learning. The environment was unique and picturesque with green tress and flowers nearly always in bloom.

Now I understand that this isn't the opportunity all of us have when we are younger, but that's just the point. It doesn't matter where we are coming from. What matters is where we are going and how we get there.

There are many incidents from my own past that perhaps can mirror the lives of others. But the question remains, what is there from our past that can re-inform our lives? This can be something simple, something innocent or again something real, like the beauty of nature. Certainly there are handfuls of aspects and attributes from those years that are no longer functioning parts of daily routine. Some may have escaped us for a while and others may take consistent work to adeptly reapply. Either way, tangibles from the past can become fortuitous parts of life today.

John Travolta was probably one of the biggest names during the 1970s. Disco was also really big and with it, rock 'n' roll. We listened to Elton John, The Rolling Stones, The Beatles, Jackson Browne, David Bowie, Peter Frampton, Bruce Springsteen, Joe Walsh, Genesis, Foreigner, Fleetwood Mac. Yes, Ted Nugent, The Clash, Billy Joel, Led Zeppelin, Three Dog Night, The Fifth Dimension, and the list of several eras of greats lives on. These were just the musical talents that came of age by the late 1970s.

Do you remember how important we decided music was when we were younger? That it moved the soul? Music also chronicles a particular era in a way that no other art form can. When we add lyrics to a song, we document expressionist dealings and perspectives, often in very candid or insightful ways.

Listen to the lyrics of a few of the songs written during the 1960s, 1970s or 1980s, whichever style might suit you best. Make certain to listen to the words. Listen to several soloists or groups and to up to five favorite songs from an era. Now meditate on the words in those songs. How or why could they influence your perspectives? How might they have influenced you if you were alive at the time? What is the difference between now and then in terms of impression? What is the difference in terms of import?

Have you allowed time to slip by without taking into account its truer meaning. Have you disregarded some of the important lessons, or worse, ignored the signposts that might have led you to take a different path in life? In many lives, this will be the case. Like many of the lessons that we have learned in life, they have been forgotten or ignored. Soon they are replaced by more selfish desires or, again worse, the cares, trials and tribulations of the world. Has the world supplanted your innermost desires and feelings in time? Take a few moments to think carefully.

The decade of the 1970s offered the opportunity for creative innovation and expression that I believe has contributed much to formation for youth of today. For instance, freedom or liberation became much more a way of life, not just an ideal.

I was a young boy when John F. Kennedy and Martin Luther King, Jr. were assassinated, but was in high school during the Watergate scandal. There were gas shortages, typewriters and phones that still dialed by turning the knob with your finger. I also remember when doctors would come to your home to make 'house calls.' The local bakery would also come to your home to make fresh deliveries.

High school is a chance to experience, to share and become part of something if you choose to. It's a chance to be curious, observant, wild, sane or insane, addictive or non-addictive, comfortable or uncomfortable with or without others. It was during the 1970s and still is now.

My first experiences were not only looking down the big hallways and large corridors but also trying to find my locker with its appropriate combination number. Homeroom began and there were at least five Smiths, so I had to listen very attentively to get my particular class schedule straight. I felt a little anxious but no more perhaps than the next student.

New beginnings are always filled with both excitement and worry. In fact apprehension is often an integral part of the excitement, itself. "There is nothing to fear but fear itself," often becomes very real, is never cliché and offers respite from worry when something new and important arises in our lives. Accepting change for the better is a right action and takes courage as well as promise.

My English teacher wore large wide-rimmed glasses. She told us that we would be reading two books a month and the class looked rather frightened. Then, she played a record on the turntable. She told us to identify what she was playing and write an essay about the lyrics as well as what the music meant to us individually. I'll always remember that experience as being unique and can understand that the teacher was asking us to share each of our true insights with her.

To impart the wisdom associated with good lessons and learning while embracing others and teaching healthy practices as well as good attributes is called sharing. Sharing positive energy is not just good, it's actually great. All parties benefit from giving, which still and will remain better than receiving.

My English teacher at the time explained that literature, "Is a way of becoming a thinker, being original and getting into the personality of characterization." Our first book was *The Old Man in the Sea* by Ernest Hemingway. She asked the class to pick a character from the book and act out what he or she was experiencing and feeling. We were to pick the part of the book that interested us the most.

This particular teacher not only knew the importance of feelings, but she demonstrated the value of sharing by engaging the class in special activities as a group. Learning became an exercise in how to act not react.

The next class was history. The teacher would dash into the room with a pronounced degree of enthusiasm. We called him Mr. T. He would walk around the room asking the students to explain what history meant to each one of them. As he did, he used his tie as if it were a microphone, like a live radio or T.V. broadcast announcer might do.

Arriving at my desk, he once asked, "Smitty, what does Gandhi have to share with us that is relevant to society today?" I replied that he offered a vision and then I spoke about the word 'suffering,' as well as what the notions of peace and democracy meant to the world.

He then explained his own stories about Horatio Alger and Sr. Thomas Moore. He presented views of utopia, explained what utopia might really mean and then asked if we could carry this insight into contemporary society.

Can you remember your own historical heroes? Who were they? Are they still your heroes? If not, why? Have they been replaced by more contemporary heroes, or do they just seem more ordinary with time?

Remember your first impressions of a utopian society? Have they changed? Do you live in a utopian world? Why not? Not only should we progress toward our own personal utopias but we should also learn how to contribute some of its benefits to society at large.

A teacher dedicated to his field, Mr. T. recognized the goodness in all his students. He also dared to explain that each student had his or her own given potential. He believed that hard work and dedication were the only ways to fulfill lifelong dreams. "With persistence," he exclaimed, "you can move mountains."

Have you ever had a teacher that made an impact on your life or one that you remember for a specific good reason? There are still many Mr. T's left in the world and hopefully there will be many more. Teachers are often select idealists. That's why many become teachers.

I started the first fitness, karate and martial arts club at school. We began with simple stretching exercises and the students were taught about proper posture and balance, aerobic fitness and endurance. We also worked on basic stances, punches, kicks, blocks, and systematic patterns of movements called 'katas.' While students liked pairing up with each other to practice techniques, there was something more important that they enjoyed. Meditation.

There is a need for stillness and calmness through meditation in karate. For students at the time it was really a first-hand approach to an important underlying principal of karate training, which is based upon focus and concentration. If student minds remain uncluttered until sessions are through, thought processes become more balanced, tranquil and quiet.

We also discussed values, higher qualities and what living attributes like humility and better character really meant. Importantly, we discussed the need to share those characteristics with others for their own betterment.

# Phil Tisi
# History Teacher, Suffern High School

*There is more pressure on kids today then ever before, including the new standardized tests. The major difference is the home. I think that when you were growing up Teddy, the living environment was much more stable and in many cases today it's totally dysfunctional.*

*Schools can't become social service agencies and we as teachers can't take the place of the parents. My father said to me once that education begins at the dinner table. That's one of the most profound lessons in life that we learn. Today there is no dinner table. Today there is a computer, and a trip to the fast food restaurant; that's dinner. And, schools can't make up for that.*

*There is a renewed desire for the sense of community today. People are tired of being de-personalized and being part of strip malls and huge malls. People want a feeling of togetherness and I think that 9/11 has a lot to do with it.*

*If you don't understand the past you're bound to make mistakes in the present. You have to teach people to be more deliberative and analytical. Success in life is a combination of inspiration and perspiration. I'm constantly trying to give my students the idea that self-fulfillment means a lot and tell them not to listen to people when they say, 'You can't do this,' or 'You can't do that.'*

*People like you Teddy became self-actualized. If you listened to people say, 'You can't do this,' or 'You cant do that,' you wouldn't have done anything in your life. I try to get students involved and have them pursue their own dreams. You need more dreamers and people willing to take risks. The world is not getting simpler for kids; it's getting more complex.*

*When I speak to my classes, I tell my students about Teddy Smith who I had as a student at Suffern High School. I say that he was an enthusiastic guy and was never afraid to take a risk. You weren't afraid.*

*Today people don't try; they don't even make an attempt. You always tried. You win some; you loose some for the next experience. Keep writing and keep moving on.*

*Phil Tisi*

# Chapter Five

Did you suspect years ago that you would be doing the things you are doing today? If you could re-live your youth do you think your current perspectives would change? In other words, it is important to understand on how true and firm a foundation your present life and lifestyle is based.

I used to bang out tunes on our high school radio station similar to the way I play music on popular stations today. Then it was Pink Floyd, Led Zeppelin, Carole King, and Cat Stevens.

The Library Director once ran into the station room and we locked the door behind him. Good humor is a positive attribute and a key to success throughout life.

Vinyl records and turntables were all there at the time. As DJ for the radio club I just kept spinning great tunes. I would talk between the songs, talk up the vocals, talk back the songs, and give great concert tips for the upcoming events at the Community College Field House. These concerts included notables such as Peter Frampton, Pegasus, Styx, and Billy Joel.

Many of us love music. It moves our soul. What was unique about the radio club? It was a free forum with no format. Play what you want, when you want.

"We are now playing the best renditions of Peter Paul and Mary, Asia, Journey, Kenny Rogers, and Crystal Gayle to start us off." It was all meant to inform as well as entertain. And, I was also recognized as a leader or even a hero of 'the movement.'

Life is a continuum, a journey. It is a process of feeling, realization, destiny, fate, and interconnectivity. Life can also change in a moment. Beliefs can change by experience or through environmental adjustment. But, paths can be altered by simple curiosity.

Sometimes it takes just a gesture of acknowledgement to make it all worth while. When was the last time you acknowledged the accomplishment of a peer? Do you think through time's journey how important acceptance was to you? What could ever make us think that it means any less to someone else today?

We should take a moment every once in a while to acknowledge someone else's accomplishment, especially simple ones. Then, try the same exercise several times a day for several days in a row. You'll shortly recognize the difference it can make in yourself as well as others.

The morning school announcements sparked the drive and provided me with the confidence to pursue commercial radio and television. I'm a proponent of change and when it's time to move on you move on. Soon I was pursuing and securing employment at well known broadcast stations. It was positive reinforcement that I received from other students that helped me learn not only take pride in my work, but also the importance of recognizing other people's accomplishments along the way.

Wrestling was another positive activity that brought me personal and eventually professional satisfaction. Wrestling is a demanding sport. You not only learn how to drop weight quickly, but also how to quickly pin your opponent down if you can. Workouts are fierce and strenuous and you have to think quickly. Otherwise, you'll get dropped yourself without a second's notice.

Life in general is equally demanding. Today these demands begin when we are young. Yesterday, this wasn't always so.

As adults, we have to think constantly: driving a car, crossing a street, admonishing a stranger, riding a bike, cooking a meal, writing a letter, or even sending an e-mail. So much depends on the accuracy of the simplest tasks. Yet, how often do we realize that our lives can actually depend on the outcome of these events? Talking on a cell phone while driving, crossing against the light, starting an argument, running a red light on a bike, not turning off the oven when you leave the house, using poor grammar in a correspondence, issuing an impulsive e-mail or text message, all these actions can have negative or even dire effects. And, they can negatively impact others. At such times, we can get taken down very fast. Maybe, even end up in jail. Does it really matter? Think quick!

The wrestling weigh-in was interesting because this was where it was decided who would wrestle who and who would end up benched. How do we measure up to our peers? This should always be both a question and a challenge.

Wrestling teaches you mental toughness and great physical stamina. The matches are exciting to take part in and also to watch, especially in the heavyweight division. When the wrestlers deck each other, you can hear the mat clamor with that definitive loud bang.

In life it still is the bigger you are, the harder your fall. That's why compassion helps at all levels. It can reduce the mistakes of inappropriate challenge or make the landing a little easier for someone who comes crashing down in any given situation.

Workouts are always fierce but once completed, there is a great feeling of relief. In the same way one can get a great sense of fulfillment and gratification by participating in an activity or club. The actual competition is within yourself: how much you want to strive to achieve or what your ultimate goals become. Importantly, how much energy are you willing to give to the experience? Whether it's golf, chess, a bridge team, or black jack, these tournaments can be grueling! Are you prepared to loose? All engaged will except for a specific team, or one.

High school is just another part or phase of who you are at a given stage in life. But, it can encompass a myriad of emotions, dreams, insecurities, passions, wanting to feel popular or part of a group, sharing a meaningful experience, growth through coursework, implementation of a suggested theory, or understanding new practice.

High school is an educational as well as social experience. There were always exciting parties and dances outside on the patio of each other's houses, often with live bands. The cars just lined up along the lawns.

Parties, get-togethers and even clubs can certainly merit positive experience because they develop communication and socialization skills. All types from various backgrounds gather together: wild individuals, intellectuals, nerds, jocks, artists, musicians, outcasts, cheerleaders, clowns, and other theatrically-oriented people.

Can you be a person without having to belong to a group? Are you able to socialize with all types of people? It is so important to remain an individual without having the need to become part of a clique or group. That means to somehow understand that you can always remain yourself. Many people have lost touch with themselves and have stopped understanding at one point or another who they really are. The right professional or even just a true friend can help prepare you in life for an objective self-opinion. Is there any other?

# Chapter Six

Nothing should ever really stand in your way and you don't have to prove anything to anyone else unless you choose to do so. We should also be able to get along with everyone and talk to anyone from any background no matter who we are. It doesn't matter who the other person is. Everyone is special and each one of us has something special to offer.

Of course some people are more developed or evolved than others, either physically, mentally, socially, spiritually, or intellectually. Some have more money, some less. Some are powerful, others famous. The irony is that people who have less intellectual capacity, physical capacity, or monetary means, are often happier than those who have more. Somehow they have learned to be content with who they are and what they have. Even the most unassuming of individuals can foster a wealth of personal and professional power within by reaching a higher state of overall spiritual development in their lives.

I've always been a positive person, listening to what people have to say, whether it is to share an idea, a joke, a story, or a meditation. Positive energy is a cornerstone for the development of good behaviors in life.

It should never matter what socioeconomic background you are from. In present times we regrettably have a greater division between the haves and have-nots. There are so many ways to assist other people who are in need: food programs, hospital programs, church programs, government programs, charitable organizational programs, educational programs. There are so many organized ways that an individual can contribute time and effort or financial support to a cause to help the less fortunate. Suddenly others are on a path that includes happiness that they may have otherwise not been able to travel before.

What is also special in life is a supportive family. We are blessed when we have a wonderful father and mother who believes in everything good for which we strive. Many of us still have one or both parents alive and together. Some have more than one set of parents because of the high frequency of divorce, at least in Western society. It is important to respect and praise your parents as well as other family members no matter how near, related or far away they might be.

It is also important when we look back to take the time to think of what it was like when we were younger with our parents. For those of us who have had troubled youths, or grew up without one or both parents, this could be difficult. However, our familial relationships from years ago still hold keys to future relationships with others.

What is it about family life in the past that has changed or is missing today? Other than the obvious changes in age and location, what about the nature of the relationships? Was there a certain bond, a shared secret or a tradition that is no longer present? Could life be improved if there was more closeness to them or other loved ones? Could those past values, or lack of values, be re-kindled or changed to encourage more fulfilling family units? Could you create trans-generational bonds by building bridges or creating pathways between older and younger members of your family, among your friends or just in your life, itself? These questions really should be reflected upon one-by-one and then answered in a positive frame of reference.

If the quality of your life is satisfactory at work and at home but there is even one prevailing negative family issue, it can spill over into your overall quality of life in general, affecting everything adversely. The power or influence, good or bad, of family in our daily lives is very strong. This is why familial relationships need to be objectively understood, respected, cherished, and positive.

Life when we were younger was definitely simpler because we didn't have all the technology and distractions that we have today. Many never expected so much in the way of material things. There was television, radio, books, house, clothing, and good movies to see five minutes away at a local theatre. Individuals enjoyed this simplicity and some have tried to keep that way of life.

However, in today's society, it is very easy to get caught up in frivolous alternatives. Cell phones, videos, TV, digital cameras, DVDs, CDs, micro-cassette recorders, voice mail messages, e-mails, text messages, and so many other activities can become overpowering and even have very negative effects in our lives. Try eliminating or reducing the inordinate use of one or more of the above that isn't vital for life or career per day until you've eliminated and diminished the use of as many as you can. Now, how long can you live without the distraction? Substitute the time with good behaviors such as exercising, reading a good book, prayer, meditation, or developing a hobby, perhaps one that you enjoyed in your youth. Reducing time spent in any 'distracting' activities and replaced with contemplative rest, prayer or meditation can help provide you and those around you with increased serenity, peace and an overall increased quality of life.

Friendship in the past often remained more constant. I can still pick up the phone today and speak with many of my friends whether we last spoke yesterday or twenty years ago. Life today is so much more complex and time for friendships has dwindled. I know that we can still uphold principles like love, humility and compassion, even when things become distracting and difficult. However, it was a lot easier years ago for people to focus on values and ethics and then share the fruits of these attributes with others as friends.

As I grew up, I was taught that belief in God was fundamental. Faith in God and humankind has always played an important role in my development. It's a primary part of the Judeo-Christian ethic and very much a part of the spiritual concepts upon which many other Eastern and Western belief systems are based. When these beliefs aren't taught or acquired in youth, it can become much more difficult to learn or develop later in life.

It's difficult enough to keep true values in perspective in contemporary times. Add the distractions, and suddenly faith in higher belief systems, prayer, meditation, human development, and even love of humankind can become too easily supplanted by worldly desires such as greed, avarice and pursuit of wealth or power, especially for wrong reasons.

Looking back is again vital in our program for self-development. This is because the answers to today's dilemmas are often found in the past; within us and in the world as it has evolved around us. Unraveling the years between our youth and today can unearth simple solutions to now seemingly complex problems. If religion or morality was a part of yesterday, why isn't it really a part of today? Certainly simplifying worldliness in one's life in general is a good way to make room for new attitudes as well as new positive activities.

Physical education is very important. Some of us liked school classes in this area but then again, some of us didn't. However, the truth is that some form of physical education is fundamental to physical, emotional and mental wellbeing.

Many of us ran as young adults, played in the gym or ran around the track. And, there were often cross-country events, hiking or just playing in the woods.

Floor hockey was always a challenging sport and dodge ball a fun experience. Weight training also appealed to many because you needed to understand and then exercise each part of your body on a regular basis.

Were you one of those who had your 'head in the sand' during physical education class? Do you feel today that you would have benefited more if you had taken physical education more seriously? The earlier good habits are established in life the easier it is to continue good habits in the future.

For some reason, physical education and competitive sports seem to play diminishing roles as we become adults. Yet the need to exercise becomes more apparent, and necessary, as we grow older. Going to the gym, health club or practicing calisthenics at home are especially needed for those living in major metropolises, where physical activity can be limited by virtue of space. How many of us participate in competitive sports past the college level? There's always a neighborhood schoolyard.

Physical education and physical activity directly affect everything that we do in life. They can also be the determining factors as to whether or not we stay healthy, and even alive.

To me, there is no activity in adult life that isn't positively influenced by a proper physical fitness routine. The more recent health club trends throughout America are a wonderful example of adults of all ages taking charge of their physical wellbeing. However, many individuals still do just want they want to do: walk on the treadmill, ride a bike, just swim, or cross country ski. In so doing an individual can miss the underlying educational components necessary for proper overall physical experience accomplishing these activities. Remember, each of those muscle building machines in the other room have specific purpose and intent.

You need to ask an expert and then work with him or her at least for a while to discover all the intricate aspects of body workout, body building and physical performance. Also, to correctly understand the many physical disciplines, methods and techniques that can be employed to coordinate mind and body with spiritual wholeness and overall wellbeing. But importantly, only a medical professional should establish a right tolerance level or activity group suitable to your age and state of health.

Some competitive sports can remain an alternative as part of an overall wellness program as one continues in life. Soccer is still of great benefit and can help to get you in shape. Shooting the ball into the goal requires great precision and skill. The game is also a good way to exhibit sportsmanship as you practice passing, blocking and trapping the ball with others.

In high school there was a unit on self-defense and then one on endurance training. Football, basketball and even swimming laps in the pool all gave you a chance to exude a high level of energy and remove frustration or hostility.

What was natural and integral then should often be part of our routines today. There are still some intrinsic physical reasons why sports activity cannot be replaced by exercise at a gym. Physical competition, balance, agility, strategy, mind-body connection, sportsmanship, and the elements of properly dealing with chance are all fundamental to overall physical fitness and wellbeing. Sports develop our abilities in these and many other areas of activity.

As young adults some physical education opportunities are enjoyed more by certain students, while other students prefer art or drama. There are many ways of acting out problems and building stamina. However, there is no exact substitute for educated physical fitness.

New adventures in high school never ceased to amaze me. Not feeling the need to be part of a group also allowed me to experience varied activities. Not being pressured by a group into participating in activities that might prove detrimental is of extreme importance, especially in today's society. Learning the value of true friendship is also a time-honored practice.

Along with family, and sometimes even in place of certain family, friends are integral to our social experience. Unlike group participation, friendship is a one-on-one stimulation in terms of growth that is both familial and nurturing. It encourages love, sacrifice and endurance in emotional as well as situational circumstances that can enrich lives. Mutual growth is what fosters good society and encourages social development for groups at a higher and more mutually beneficial physical, mental and spiritual level.

I once had a friend named Al. We used to go to Rolling Stones and Bruce Springsteen concerts together. He was a unique person. What made him unique was his honesty, love for people and sense of humor. There was nowhere that we would go without having a good laugh.

We could be enjoying a rock concert, sitting at his parents' house for a good home cooked meal or even eating at a local diner. Wherever we were, he could find the opportunity to comment on the insanity of life. He took each incident very seriously, but knew that we were only here for a short stay. He in particular always understood that we often make situations in life more serious or intense than they should be at any given point in time.

You didn't have to worry about what you said around Al. He never judged anyone and never really cared about what people thought or said because he was never judgmental or status-seeking.

Times spent with those we cherish should be like times spent with Al. A sense of humor is always welcome and encouraged in human interaction. Then, in the seriousness of repose, one is better re-disposed to the elements of fortitude, rectitude and forgiveness.

Experience is still one of the greatest teachers. The value of experiences, personal or situational, positive or negative, can be applied and reapplied throughout life. Many people do not always understand that experience is also informational. They refuse to get past the moment to realize that several moments later the experience can be gone. If it was a negative experience, it can eventually be forgiven or forgotten. However, if it was positive, it should be treasured like a natural pearl discovered and then saved for enrichment. Just like a good friend.

I've realized that to be a successful and interesting teacher you have to be able to draw from a wellspring of knowledge and experiences that relate to your own as well as other's situations. Remembering what it was like to be a student yourself can also enrich the teaching process.

We all come in different packages and with more or less different baggage. Some individuals are extremely complex, some deeper in meaning or intent, some more sensitive, some less sensitive, some very warm, and some very cold. I feel strongly that everyone has their own story to tell. Each one has hidden treasure inside their body, mind, spirit, and soul. Some are in touch with that very special something that lies within. Others are blinded by their own intellect, or self-centered or even narcissistic, all of course in detrimental ways.

Prayer and meditation become doors that open into worlds of growth and understanding. Spirituality and aspiring to the greater virtues is the firmest of all foundations upon which we can and should build our lives and beliefs.

'Reality' is a word that we think we understand. We know that we can hear, touch, see, smell, and feel from our five senses. Although this is only natural, it still needs to be properly understood. I would then explain that there are a handful of other dimensions that are less tangible but can come to or through us in significant ways. To deny the reality of something that we can't fully understand or need to learn more about to better comprehend is an act of ignorance as well as disbelief. Through faith and with hope we can find true understanding.

Can we really exercise control over our lives? Yes. To what extent? That answer differs from person to person.

Life deals us all different cards, different sets of circumstances and challenges, providing us with different means to resolve personal, professional and social issues. It sends us in different directions, whether it is physical, mental, emotional, professional, financial, or spiritual. It also sends us mixed signals.

Life is change. Change is life. Life is also a mystery. So is afterlife. Truly understanding life and afterlife is an art. It requires wisdom, understanding, piety, knowledge, fortitude, counsel, and the fear of God. It also draws from a number of other spiritual gifts, human disciplines and practices. When combined, studied and practiced simultaneously the virtues gained from attuning oneself to a higher sense of learning and being creates a greater sense and appreciation of life. It also reveals patterns for self-improvement that can be well-applied again toward others.

This is why I feel unraveling the mysteries of life is greater than just an experience. The proper practice of physical, mental and spiritual disciplines unleashes tremendous power. The implementation of good practices and good works from that power becomes an art in and of itself.

My assistant principal in high school, Dr. Woodward, was someone you could never forget because he held fast to the qualities that hold strong in almost any life today. He also worked consistently for the improvement of others. He walked around the school extending individualized encouragement to students and cheering them on.

He often smiled and had a great sense of humor. He would provide a personal joy that made us want to go to school and belong. He could also find that special quality in a person and bring out the best in each individual.

Dr. Woodward always showed a personal interest in a student's potential. He wanted the best for each and every student and would exclaim, "Dare to care!"

Between phases or even situations in life, one has to find the time to understand who they really are and how it relates to their understanding of others. In other words, one has to care. Without care and understanding for one's self as well as others there is no bridge between each of our lives.

If we have goals to achieve in life that remain a mystery, then certainly unraveling that mystery is of primary importance. Taking time to comprehend the richer meanings that unfold during daily experience helps to make the happenstance of time unveil as a unified and purposeful program.

The high school library is significant to everyone and for me was a great place to not only find a few moments of respite but also come to terms with everyday occurrences. The picture windows faced the beautiful outdoors with the woods and mountains surrounding the school making it conducive to accomplish homework assignments or prepare reports. The mood was so calm that you could always spend time reflecting as well as thinking about the future.

Is there a special place in your own life that you can retire and contemplate? Where is that place? Is it inside yourself and attainable nearly anywhere when you are alone? Or, is it at home, in a library, a park, a church, in a bedroom, boardroom, playroom, garden, neighboring wooded area, or den? Go there and be there often, because a significant attribute in your quality of life program beckons.

A child in his or her own room is not unlike an embryo in a womb. Similarly, the proper environment for an adult fosters positive growth and development.

The ability to be alone and remain content can also shelter us from 'peer pressure' at any age. Refusing to compromise in the face of negative or dangerous activity is necessary in life and builds stamina as well as develops character for the future.

Did you have the ability in your youth to say no in situations involving others, even if it led to ostracism or out-and-out rejection? Importantly, do you have that ability today?

The memories and positive attributes experienced during high school still feel as if they were just taught yesterday. Memory can be quite profound, but so can time and imagination.

Have you ever thought about where you would be if you turned the clock back five, fifteen or twenty-five years? Then, purposefully set out to do whatever it was you needed to do simply because you enjoyed the goodness in the experience at the time? What would you really want out of life if you had the chance to relive just a part of it? Is that still an attainable goal today?

We should be willing to work hard and then properly accomplish new beginnings with new goals and objectives. This means identifying or discovering which path or road would we need to switch to make up for any lost time. Do you feel that you are on the right path already? Time can change nearly anything, and if you choose wisely, especially for the best.

*Alfonso Renna, Teddy Smith and Kevin (Oz) Osborn*

# Chapter Seven

Training your body so that it stays in shape and remains limber throughout life is a challenge. Balance and timing are significant in each of our daily activities. Knowing how much, recognizing too little or too much, pacing activities, and fully understanding the benefits of balance and good timing when also applied to individual experiences can enrich those experiences and positively influence outcomes.

In terms of growth and development there are several distinct stages in life processes and one of them unquestionably ends after high school. This is when many youths leave their family and homes and begin to learn independence. However, the value systems that are developed until such time have a way of influencing years to come.

There should be elements of simplicity in adulthood with roots that existed during youth. Value and belief systems often need to already be in place and should be supported through education. However, society, including family and friends, is an integral part of our development and guides us through good times, bad times, hardships, perils, the known, and the unknown. It's all a matter of time, and again, change.

How much change is necessary and good? How much in the past has proven detrimental? We should have continued to evolve, grow and become enriched. This is the time to stop and reflect upon past changes, because from here on the rate of change speeds up and shortly brings us back to the present.

Determinably, life itself becomes the ultimate education. It is a true test of the mind, body, spirit, and soul connection. We are all part of the universal evolutionary process. That process is a continual journey of truth, knowledge and the unknown.

Life is a continuum, a process and an evolution that can lead down many different roads. It's a traveling time machine, filled with experiences, thoughts, places, names, and dates, all encapsulated and stored within one's mind as well as in the minds of others.

My first post-graduate challenge was to get up and stand in front of a television camera to announce station breaks as well as to be the television announcer for a South Florida station. Being involved with television was quite an experience. Unlike school, it became learning by doing. I had never before read a cue card or looked into a teleprompter to state or explain someone else's ideas.

Media conditioning can not only program our attitudes and attributes but also steer the direction of much of our lives. Newspapers, radio, television, film, video, and the Internet not only provide information but strongly influence perspectives. Many of us are unaware of the positive or negative cumulative effects media has and can actually have upon us.

Much of a quality of life program needs to separate our self from the complexities and perplexities of media hype. This process is not meant to distance us but to put us in better touch with the reality of personal and professional experiences. Any reprogramming in our lives can only be accomplished on our own accord, on our volition and without potentially tainted perspectives that can either deter or defer us from our own particular goals and ambitions.

Sometimes both personal and professional objectives are first decided upon years prior. To many it was exciting going to work after high school because of how encompassing it all really was. For me many hours were spent in the master control room, seeing and learning about the importance of camera, switching, audio, commercials, production, and watching on-air talent. Studio producers explained when to smile at the camera and when to look more serious.

The programs were formatted so that there was live talk alternating with prerecorded on-air broadcasting. We were taught what it meant to be good communicators and facilitate good discussions. We learned what it meant to give people what they wanted, or thought they needed, and keep the interview process organized, interesting and in tandem with the format of the show. We also learned the importance of not discussing personal business with employees or superimposing our own perspectives and objectives upon others, especially on-air.

Effective communication is not only a cornerstone for developing proper personal relationships but it is also essential for developing proper business relationships. Understanding and relating to the needs and desires of others is fundamental to ensuring ongoing communication that is mutually beneficial in business.

Many work related experiences, especially in larger urban areas, are also sales related. Sales are an integral and pervasive part of the capitalist experience. Good sales begin with effective communication. Good communication begins with not only an adequate understanding and appraisal of a situation but also the ability to take into consideration the needs and desires of others. Television like any other business is not just smiles and handshakes, but knowledge, talent and developing well-established relationships. It can also help to provide a balance between subjective and objective perspective in a recognized and sustainable forum.

In America, we are blessed with a host of educational experiences developed in many size and shapes. In addition to formal education that leads to graduate and post-graduate degrees, there are continuing education programs sponsored by schools and other institutions, organizations and corporations nationwide. Many involve real-life experiences and address all areas of curriculum, philosophies, business, and importantly communication from a multitude of approaches that embrace practical experience.

Do you feel that you have reached the end of your own educational resources? Perhaps you should rethink the situation and research continuing education that can support your current or prospective initiatives. Remember, there is always time enough to simply continue or especially, learn how to effectively begin again. Applied properly to life, education becomes real in practice, creates further balance and harmony and can positively effect the challenge of change.

# Chapter Eight

It is important to be and remain a self-motivated learner. A school called Hampshire College located in Amherst, Massachusetts, offered that particular type of education in a suitable environment that seemed to best suit my temperament. Hampshire College is located in the New England countryside surrounded by the most beautiful farms, fields and forests. Like the surrounding rainbows of changing colors patterned by the leaves on an autumn afternoon, Hampshire offered a multifaceted continuing education experience. Both the setting and school were conducive to learn, grow and expand emerging horizons.

There were dogs running to-and-fro as well as students sun tanning on the college grounds. Students came from all over the world to attend this school because it was one of the foremost institutions of higher education that attracted creative self-motivated learners. To me, it was a school where one could organize his or her own program and develop a curriculum with moderated discretion. The campus also had a great gym, physical fitness center, beautiful swimming pool, and a first class art and dance center.

Unlike other colleges, we were required to write papers but it wasn't necessary to take ongoing examinations. Here, you weren't judged by your ability to perform on a stringent standardized basis. Instead, you only needed to pass three division exams to graduate. You were assigned a committee of two professors that would evaluate the quality of your work. There would be an extensive oral discussion where you would have to defend your coursework, papers, research, and off-campus internships.

Work environments in the adult world should be starting points for continuing education in life. Not all of us have the beauty of nature at the doorsteps of our place of employment but today many do. This can stimulate reflection and offer temporary respite for new thoughts and ideas to emerge.

In more urban work settings surrounding architecture provides artistic repose. Finding a niche physical environment at or around the workplace, urban or suburban, can encourage personal and professional reflection and ensuing advancement.

Developing a self-sustaining educational curriculum based upon self-motivation can become less difficult in the work or business environment than developing purely self-motivational models during the education process. Additionally, many jobs also offer the opportunity for on or off-site training and professional development for employees. This is a great place to again learn.

If you are in a more competitive executive or professional situation, outreach for knowledge to give you that edge on others in your field is also a prudent beginning. Licenses, certifications and continuing education degrees will not only give you new building blocks upon which to build your career but also provide very needed feelings of self-fulfillment that may be lacking in the workplace itself. This self-fulfillment becomes an added self-motivation to build a professional curriculum yourself to enrich your own work experience and hopefully the lives of others in the process.

In order to survive Hampshire College you needed to understand how to be independent, disciplined, conscientious, and above all, a consistent self-learner. I've always enjoyed challenges and new experiences. Hampshire offered me that length, depth and added breadth of opportunity to acquire significant knowledge. It also enabled me to re-present creative concepts, connect ideas and make valuable associations as they relate to overall academic study as well as practical real-world situations among others.

Again, not all students have had the opportunity to benefit from as liberal an education as was developed and implemented at Hampshire College. However, it would be foolish to assume that such an education can not become a way of life in the postgraduate world. Challenges of independence will be at least as rigorous tomorrow as they are today. All educational and scholarly improvement can provide the wherewithal to meet continuing challenges in life that are necessary for development and advancement.

Attempting to learn outside the comfort zone can help turn challenges into an education. Learning beyond one's immediate threshold of endurance can result in surprisingly unique developments. New knowledge gained and adeptly applied to an uncomfortable business environment or career path will change your professional circumstances enough to make it not only endurable but again a base for further personal and professional expansion.

Certainly we can look back and also find singular educational experiences that had profound impact on us. Those simple insights can become fundamental in many ways for today's growth and future development.

I'll always remember one of my first classes in economics where the professor combined both micro and macro-economics in one course. This was challenging as well as exhilarating. The class opened my eyes to multiple-related assignment and multiple-task initiatives.

In today's complex and rigorously ordained society, multiple-task implementation is a must to successfully accomplish daily activities. The ability to successfully work simultaneously on several projects, or for those more singularly minded in work ethic accomplishment, alternate between different given programs, is a gift. Diversity in work experience helps to eliminate the stumbling blocks of repetition and similitude in professional exercise.

Time can also be a continuum issue that confronts job related scenarios. It is important to understand that nothing can improve the assemblage and maintenance of time better than pacing. It is necessary to recognize the value of pacing to properly accomplish given and ongoing goals and objectives.

At Hampshire we were allowed to work at our own pace without any pressure from either the professor or peers. I quickly found that freedom allowed me to become more involved with work in a more fulfilling experiential way. It was better to utilize time properly and truly enjoy the learning process as it unfolded. Not having to worry about short-term understanding or memorization of inordinate details for tests eliminated the pressure to learn at anyone else's pace and allowed greater understanding of exercises at the practical level.

When you feel undue pressure in your work it becomes difficult to make proper connections between your job and personal experience. It is overall experience that becomes the best teacher and the better motivator for learning the power of developing a happier life. Without informational as well as inspirational experience in at least a somewhat free environment, work and life can become stagnant or at the least, limited dimensional exercises.

How is your learning or work experience connected to your life? It can often be something that you enjoy and that spills over into more personal activities. It should also be something that you feel is invigorating and comfortable to share with family and friends, neighbors or even strangers. Is there connectivity to it at all? If there isn't, then there needs to be a quick reappraisal of the work program and either the addition of connecting factors like developmental learning or even just changing work environments. The microcosmic work environment must have valued and simultaneous connectivity to the macrocosmic experiences of life itself. Otherwise, stagnation, isolation or even reversal of the growth process can ensue. No matter what the job experience might be, creating order out of chaos, truth from understanding or right from wrongful experiences is an art that can be transferred from professional into personal life.

Evaluating learning, relating it to other learning and then applying it to real life disciplines is practice that I apply with my students today. Discipline and perseverance are also fundamental to educational, physical education, sports, and martial arts programs. Likewise, these aspects of learning are applicable to all work processes and the creating of proper relationships throughout a lifetime.

College taught me how to turn negative challenges into positive ones. If you want something that you believe in enough then pursue it fervently. You'll need a mindset sustained by discipline and proper follow-through to truly persevere. Nothing can or will stop you from achieving what you really put your mind to do if it is right and good for you in the grander scheme. You just need to be as strong as possible, mentally and physically, to be able to move forward. And, be in tune with an overriding spiritual good that is the driving force and power of all.

Self-confidence and strong will can be gained through meditation or prayer. Strength will overcome weakness just as surely as good ultimately overcomes evil. A sense of discipline means remaining structured especially in a free environment and centered on what you do by giving as much as you can to what you believe in.

Always try your best and put your heart into what you feel is right. In doing so, you will become strengthened by life experiences and will have learned through each and every meaningful act. This will encourage you to continue to learn, persevere, grow, and prosper.

# Chapter Nine

Hampshire College is part of a five college consortium. With four other schools in the Northeast, students had the opportunity to take classes on different campuses. One school was a well-known and then predominantly women's school called Mount Holyoke College. There I studied anthropology.

The foundations of learning coordinated during college years are cornerstones for post-graduate education. They can become steppingstones for expanding well-grounded and objective pathways in life. Throughout the world and even in America many have not or will not have the opportunity to accomplish higher education. Yet, simply understanding a handful of the disciplines and course structures of education at the higher level can provide a road map for learning in or out of an organized educational environment.

Experiences at Mount Holyoke taught me the value of relating to women in a class. Being the only male, including the professor, was something that might once have been quite uncomfortable but actually became enjoyable. Learning about other cultures in an all female class was truly unique. At Mount Holyoke men were significantly outnumbered so I had to be careful about what I said and did. This helped teach me humility, respect for the opposite sex and how to exercise self-control in differing situations.

In the often male-dominated world of business men can forget how women might feel in a given professional circumstance. In the instance of sexual harassment men prove uncaring and unreasonable. Such actions are always uncalled for and also, illegal.

Conversely, some women feel a need to compete with their sexual counterparts in a male frame of reference. Certainly in some professions a false sense of competition can be a defense mechanism in response to male pressure. In reality, the difference between the sexes harbors a promise for relationships that transcend equality. It is the difference that holds attraction and I am convinced that it is in the difference that there is a promise for mutual growth.

As we approach physical disciplines and encourage specific activities for children and adults, you'll see that expectations and outcomes change from individual-to-individual and circumstance-to-circumstance. Proper respect for the opposite sex encourages personal, professional and sociological evolution and growth.

Listening to what others have to say also kept me out of trouble. Moderating a radical position on an issue that was being studied at Mount Holyoke helped transition this particular student learning experience. This practice of listening has very positively influenced my teaching experiences at all levels of instruction.

Spending a semester at Columbia University also provided an intellectually enriching experience in the field of public speaking. Our professor gave us rigorous assignments on how to present a speech and how not to fear being in front of an audience. Think before you speak. This is a lesson that remains with me today.

It is also amazing how you can lose the fear factor by simply attempting something that you once thought was too difficult. By adding practice you can earn the confidence and gain the will necessary to continue without fear.

Learning becomes more enjoyable when an objective teacher is well-prepared and can intelligently relate subject matter to current or world events. Public speaking classes are particularly inspiring because a speech can convey a particular message that is readily appreciated by others. The satisfaction of others becomes a great personal accomplishment.

Respect is a two-way street and when it is given as well as received it proves quite fulfilling. Being able to bring a class or one's peers into a situation by effectively expressing feelings or perspectives allows for mutual growth. It also encourages respect.

Growth can also come when you rid yourself of the negative aspects of ego, that part within one's self that prevents us from moving forward, accepting new people at face value, embracing new situations, and ultimately accumulating new and useful knowledge. If you want to attempt an exercise to help remove false ego, take a large pitcher, fill it to the top with water, close your eyes, and say, "I want to get rid of the excess baggage and clutter in my life. I need to become other than self-centered, properly focused and rid myself of negative experiences." Then, open your eyes and completely empty the pitcher. Now, close your eyes once more and offer a prayer of hope and willingness to learn things that you have not learned before. Hope for a willingness to cleanse yourself of illusions and preconceptions, with the ability to simply surrender to a more peaceful state.

Open your eyes a second time and then think that you are ready to learn anything that is positive to your wellbeing and that you are ready to delve into your self or inner core to find a truer nature. You're now ready to learn beginning steps to new experiences filled with joy and contentment and, like a child living from moment-to-moment, with a desire to grow.

A child's mind is filled with new and innovative ideas, curiosity and openness to learning. Education is growth from new points of origin not unlike those in the life of a child. Only with simplicity of mind, empty of any preconception and confusion, can one really start along a path filled with goodness, challenge and positive reinforcement. Somewhere along that road you will begin to prosper, eventually even effortlessly. When that finally occurs, I think that you will agree you have not only unlocked the power but also have somehow tapped the art of living a more seamless and graceful life.

At Hampshire College, professors were called by their first names. This assisted in removing the stigma that placing them on a higher plateau than students can impose. It's much less intimidating and easier to relate to teachers at least to some extent as equals. Maybe even like a friend.

Equality, or at least a sense of equality, is also necessary in personal as well as hierarchal professional structures. We are never any better, or for that matter any worse, than our peers or others. Communication and equality are not disparate concepts. In fact, one borrows from as well as contributes to the other.

It's interesting to find that with communal living, on or off-campus in a more society oriented environment, exposure to diverse cuisines increases. Control of nutritional intake should become important at the earliest stages of life. Regretfully, the youth of today are at a disadvantage in terms of nutritional orientation and variation. Wholesome eating with product diversity has been replaced by fast foods. Many adults still don't maintain anything near a proper diet. Young and old alike need to unlearn their eating habits and re-learn properly balanced dietary practice. In no way does this become uninteresting. In fact, it opens the doors to a myriad of international choices and alternatives that are healthy and may eventually become fundamental to our overall wellbeing.

Regrettably, as many mature, their inclination to diversity diminishes instead of increases. Society can have a distinct way of reducing not expanding our choices. Even in the highly sophisticated, technology-driven, information-based world that we live in, people still choose to be Democrat or Republican, liberal or conservative, and often become, rich or poor, happy or sad, and disarmingly, good or evil. For some people the middle-ground seems to have disappeared.

Further narrowing our choices is a tendency to unwittingly embrace the belief systems of others, which is sometimes referred to as 'blind faith.' Lack of understanding is never a substitute for inquisitiveness. And, disinterest is a form of digression not progression.

Just like a child learns by expanding his or her boundaries, we need to mature with an open mind beginning with respect for the thoughts and desires of others. This may take new beginnings to accomplish, with a sincere heart to create a new way of life. For many it will mean learning over again how to communicate effectively. This may take a profound commitment to change within to better appreciate that which is without.

# Chapter Ten

As we continue our journey through the maturing process there are many issues and attitudes already discussed that need to be applied. Approaching daily exercises and disciplines, important aspects of the attitudes and attributes of life already discussed should begin to be incorporated into daily practice. Incorporating new beginnings as starting points in our lives opens the doors to many new areas in daily existence where good health, wellbeing and happiness can thrive.

One key to happiness that builds and sustains healthy physical, spiritual and mental growth is again, friendship. One way to develop friendships is to better understand the intricacies of socialization.

You need to maintain a balance between being serious and less serious when socializing. Relationship building at the adult level begins for many earlier in life. By the time we reach twenty-one our ability to socialize as adults should be grounded and at least a handful of social perspectives carefully considered and addressed.

Another aspect of youth that should transfer more readily into adult life as explained is expanded fitness and sports. Training, weights and exercise equipment are utilized today by many and consistently in my own personal and professional training programs.

Proper transition from youth to adulthood is based upon the theoretical and philosophical, but it becomes experiential in nature, remaining practical as well on the physical plane. I cannot stress enough that we need proper care of the body to help support and nurture growth in mental, emotional and spiritual well-being.

Transition doesn't happen overnight. It actually takes a lifetime of learning which is what makes the process so extensive but exhilarating. It takes a great deal of patience, perseverance, right action, and even rectitude to follow a more righteous path.

One of the better motivations for education in one's life should be success in studies. Not everything studied needs to have an applicable or monetary value assigned to it afterwards. In a proper frame of reference there shouldn't have to be a monetary value associated with one's vocational life. That isn't to say that you shouldn't be thinking of making a decent living or providing for loved ones. However, there needs to become established balances between the accumulation of knowledge, the application of moral values and the accumulation of wealth.

Establishing better character traits early in life is important for proper communication, ability to live with one another, acquiring lasting friendships, and establishing a suitable work environment throughout life. You can learn very much along these lines early on by studying philosophy and religion, reading good novels and self-help books and viewing films of quality and substance. However, by practicing what you acquire as knowledge with humility, patience, confidence, straightforwardness, honesty, compassion, understanding, and respect for others, including those who may or may not be as fortunate, is the most beneficial and satisfying way to go. Remembering to respect other people's feelings along this same path is the essence of improving the very necessary bond of proper association.

As I look back at my educational and other learning experiences and focus on substantial points of reference, I realize that focus and concentration eventually become paramount for success. Meditation also assisted greatly in this respect, allowing me to see and understand more clearly. This fuller experience has helped me to better appreciate the details in life and recognize the great challenges that are an ongoing test of spirit and soul.

The attitudes and attributes for proper development of the mind and body are sometimes referred to as mind, body, spirit, and soul connection. Since all of these are concurrent entities it shouldn't be a surprise to realize how one can very significantly affect the other. The higher a being you become, the more harmonious the mind, body, spirit, and soul connection are. This is always the better goal and more profound objective in life, and especially when it is shared.

There is a great sense of accomplishment graduating from college. Higher education opens one's eyes to many new ideas and experiences. At the end of a curriculum you can better understood how to think, analyze and critically appraise a body of information with commitment and meaningfulness.

It is very important to remain respectful and courteous towards faculty members and students alike. I believe strongly that this good behavior pattern goes back to the respect one has for his or her own parents or family. The way you treat others is sometimes what you witnessed as a child, or how you were treated by your parents or immediate family, and how you treated them in return.

It is hard to unlearn bad habits and bad character traits often develop in youth. As we mature, it takes much more time and effort to follow the good as opposed to the evil inclinations in life. Even more so if you haven't had practice since childhood. It takes one gradual step after another to relearn and then retrain one's ethical standards. This is very important to understand because as an adult you often have the opportunity to not only positively influence the outcome of other adults, but also of children.

Continuing education and alternative methods of learning keep the mind stimulated. Keeping your body and mind active is also the key to longevity. The more you learn the wiser you become and better able to relate to yourself and experiences in the everyday world.

Education is a lifelong practice and as explained, it doesn't have to begin or end with school. It not only develops quality of life but it expands ways to further develop meaning in life. Understanding and practicing determination, or perseverance, can replace the occasions and memories of bad experiences and improve personal abilities as well as interpersonal relationships. Perseverance is a cornerstone for pursuing leadership, developing focus and maintaining goal oriented practices.

My vision has always been to help others by showing them how to become and remain focused, sincere, honest, and forthright. This is the commitment that I attempt to make to better society, the lives of individuals and especially the lives of children. This goal has led me to understand a more compassionate way of recognizing suffering in the world and to strive to acquire better methods for positively impacting lives by helping to remove difficulties in life before they arise.

## Gregory Prince
## Former President, Hampshire College

*I think it's important to ask students to reflect, or ask them to reflect on what they're doing. And, to reflect on yourself and your life.*

*I go to high schools and ask people why they study history. I talk about the fact that history is about telling stories, and that it matters who tells the story, which story gets told and how it gets told. One way you shape the past and the future is by stories. That's the oral tradition where history began. Culture and society and civilization began with telling stories.*

*Stories were told as a way and a part of controlling destiny, controlling the future, and it's true today. It's how you tell your own story. If you tell your own story in a positive way, you have a much higher chance of having a more positive outcome. The stories you tell about yourself begin to guide the choices you make and the things you look for and the way you look at the world around you. So, thinking about the story you want to tell about yourself is beginning to shape and plot how you're going to live your life. Therefore, reflection and storytelling are very interrelated.*

*Reflection is not looking back and saying what is, quote, "the reality." It's looking back and asking, "What are the patterns that now you can see, that you couldn't see then?" That's part of the reason for reflecting.*

*When I began my career, getting out of college, I couldn't possibly have created the narrative that I now create. It's looking back.*

*I ended up in my first position out of college in The China Association, working in Hong Kong for three years teaching English, at a Chinese College. And, the second year I was there, the Chinese College was officially integrated into two other colleges, to create the Chinese University of Hong Kong. So, one of the highlights of my life was in the second year of my career, when I was a charter member of the faculty of what I hoped would be someday a great university.*

*What I found I really enjoyed was less my personal achievement and more my association with the creation of institutions. That's something I see now, but it began then, though I could not have articulated it at that time. Yale China is a very small organization. It's lasted for one hundred years and never has had a whole lot of money, but very dedicated people. It has managed in the course of that time to build a China nursing school, a medical school, a hospital, and middle school, that survived World War*

*I, World War II, the Communist Revolution, and today is one of the eight major regional medical centers in China owned and run by the Chinese. It's an extraordinary achievement that has accomplished an immense amount of good, beyond what any individual could have achieved and building institutions is a really important act, art, and it's one that our society devalues and has increasingly little language to describe. It's articulated theoretically by people like Robert Bellin, I can't remember who he quotes, but it's, "No freedom and no individualism without institutions." It's a thought that challenges faculty at Hampshire.*

*Hampshire's so individualistic, and that's the irony and the tension. We're a building, and a new kind of institution, which at its core is very anti-institutional, very individualistic and the most individualistic of all institutions, which creates this wonderful ironic tension.*

*Before I ever came to Hampshire, I began to realize that I really enjoyed shaping institutional structure. I was at Yale China when others could not be there. The Chinese were fighting the United States, and we still had some people in China. The Chinese never said that we had to go; they said that in order to stay we had to do A, B, C, or D, which was mainly build buildings.*

*It wasn't ideological or political, it was just putting more money in. And, finally Yale China decided that it couldn't afford what was being asked, but it was being asked in a very diplomatic way. We would love you to stay. But if you stay, you must do the following things. We couldn't do the following things. So they left. And when they left, they simply turned over the deeds and the documents, and explained it's yours, we give them to you. And they then decided well, they had raised a lot of money, what were they going to do? And again, they decided to build another institution. And so they looked -- they looked in Hong Kong and Taiwan, and decided that Hong Kong was a more free place.*

*They found three scholars in Hong Kong who were the pre-eminent scholars of the day. And Yale China approached them, and said we'd like you to build a facility. And they said no thank you, we want to be independent, we don't want to be controlled. And Yale China said no, we don't want to control you, we just want to support you. We'll be your alumni, until you have an alumni group, we'll be your alumni group. Lots of negotiation back and forth, it took about three years, but they finally said yes. So I think around 1955, they got the British Government to give them land in Hong Kong and they built them a college. Four years later, it was so distinguished that the British Government picked it and two other colleges to be federated into a Chinese University.*

*I arrived in 1961 for two years, and in 1962 the Chinese University officially came into being. It started a whole other university. And I found that, intuitively, exciting, and so I started looking for ways to shape and work with institutions.*

*In 1970, Dartmouth hired me right out of graduate school. They had a summer school that had three hundred students, and was losing $200,000 a year. I hadn't even finished my Ph.D. and Dartmouth College gave me the entire institution for three months, and said, do anything you want with it. It was sheer chance and luck, in one sense.*

*It was the most wonderful job. I didn't have to deal with all the big problems. I had an incredible institution. In three years I went from three hundred students and losing $200,000 to a thousand students and making money.*

*So suddenly, right out of grad school, somebody gave me the chance to do it; and to do everything. I changed all the rules; I changed all the regulations; I changed everything. I could hire the faculty; hire anybody I wanted.*

*Hampshire was created by four other institutions that believed that radical change was needed in higher education, and that institutions couldn't change themselves. This is a really interesting statement, that the only way to bring about radical change was to build a new institution. So we have the full cycle there. And in a sense, as institutions, they did bring about radical change, but they could only bring it about by building a new institution.*

*I was at Dartmouth nineteen years. I became a kind of maverick in the Dean of the Faculty office, and what I did in the Dean of the Faculty is that I built interdisciplinary programs. So, I built little institutions within the institution, and I was just the maverick. I helped create things like Women's Studies, Native American Studies, African and African-American studies, Environmental -- all the programs that now seem pretty tame, you know, in the context of Hampshire seem tame, but at Dartmouth were -- the ones that alums loved to hate.*

*I've enjoyed everything. I've been very blessed. And, the culmination is Hampshire. By luck, or whatever, I ended up at a place where I was* no longer trying to pull a rock up a hill. The way I describe the difference between Dartmouth and Hampshire is, Dartmouth I was trying to pull a rock up the hill and I was always afraid I'd slip and go down to the bottom and start over again. But, the rock is behind me. So, if I slipped, I just slipped.

Hampshire is much easier, I'm trying to steer the cart, run, stay ahead of it, run as fast as I can going downhill. It's infinitely more exciting -- and infinitely more dangerous, because the cart might just run right over me. But, it's exhilarating. And that's the way I feel.

I don't have to think of Hampshire's mission. It has a clearer mission than any institution I know. The interesting thing is, you always find that people from foundations, the question they always ask is, what is your vision for the institution? And I would always respond, that's the wrong question. So I explained, you should be asking me, "What's Hampshire's vision, and what am I going to do to help it come about?"

And I said, "This is an institution that has a mission, that has a set of values, and it has a culture. And I'm going to try."

And they said, "Well, what's your goal for Hampshire?" And I said, "My goal for Hampshire is to help it be more like itself. I don't think that I have to help realize it. It has the blueprint.

So I went to a foundation with the Chair of the Board, and the foundation said, "Well, what are you trying to do?" We got into a very intense conversation -- and we got the grant.

Hampshire inspires people. Hampshire creates a context in which all of us can feel we're working in the same direction. I'm inspired by students. I hope I can inspire some students. But, a lot of my job is to be the scratching post. I don't inspire them, I irritate them, and they sharpen their ability to think critically.

Collectively, what I really have found about Hampshire is that when push comes to shove, the students always have taken the high road. Not that all individual students necessarily take the high road; not that I don't chastise, discipline or go after some students. But, if you lay out a clear picture, they'll respond that way. Eventually they'll really focus, you know, really focus in. And the other thing is that they have a good sense of humor, for the most part.

But the converse of it is that every college and university in the United States offer what I call, with some hubris, a Hampshire education. And

*I also describe Hampshire as a 9th century institution rushing into the 10th century. We're profoundly classic, in the sense of the structure of this education, so what's radical about Hampshire is that we believe -- not all Hampshire people agree with me on this, but I think it's -- the most effective, most transforming education any student, any age, any background, that comes from any circumstance can get. That's the radical statement.*

*Dartmouth offered a Hampshire education to about one percent of the student body. We're taking one-half of one-percent of the best of the country, the best and the brightest, and we're saying that only three or four percent should do honors work. There's something wrong with the picture.*

*Hampshire's willing to invest the time. Not every student will produce honors level work, but it won't be a waste of their time; they tried.*

*Dartmouth's a great institution; I learned a lot of skills and developed a lot of theoretical frameworks there. But, Hampshire's where it's all put together.*

# Chapter Eleven

Post-graduate studies have become a professional necessity throughout the world. Following Hampshire College, my next learning endeavor was to attend Goddard College in northern Vermont. This particular school was surrounded by farms, woods and open land. Nature and open space again made it conducive to learning in a very special way. For instance, it was easy to go into the barn on campus and study, dance or do Tai Chi early in the morning. There were plenty of open fields and places to play or accomplish class work.

At the post-graduate level, if you wanted to be part of a poetry workshop, you were welcome. If you wanted to read your poetry in front of an audience, you'd also be allowed. If you needed to hold a discussion about philosophy, literature, politics, or theology, it was appreciated. If you were an artist, rock climber, sports buff, dancer, or even just someone trying to get a degree, the opportunities were there. It was all very open, meaning that you were not judged for expressing your innermost or outermost feelings or thoughts. Just on the quality of your work and right actions.

We often hear about 'back to nature' as a way to put a pause into our life and reevaluate the people, places and situations that we come in contact with ordinarily. In taking a short while to appreciate nature itself you can better appreciate the need to recreate a similar harmonious balance in life. Life is change. However, it is also balance.

At this next graduation I received a Master's degree. We all held hands as part of a self-cleansing spiritual moment as part of the ceremony. The university president was there acknowledging that he too was one of us, not above us or below us. He was right there with us in the present moment, sharing our dreams and passions with good wishes for all future success.

My subsequent learning experience at Sarah Lawrence College is what led me to teach. At the time I also had an Aikido club. We practiced tumbling and trying to use an opponent's weight and momentum against them. We did meditation, yoga stretches and practiced postures in addition to specific Aikido exercises and techniques. Students at the club enjoyed the experience of feeling calm and becoming balanced.

I've always enjoyed teaching and being a student at the same time. It is good to encourage others to not only better understand their own education, past or present, but also to continue to learn.

Most people need some form of formal or informal environment in which to learn, which is why college and post-graduate schools are beneficial to many of any age. However, there is alternative education in many forms that remains available to many.

Certainly adults can put together their own alternative education programs based upon constructive models. They can apply learning sets from previous experiences to either continuing formal education or participate in alternative adult or other self-motivated learning programs and projects.

As mentioned, being a student further informs teaching ability. This is true whether you become the teacher of students, your own training program or other types of programs. In any situation, listening to your own inner voice as well as the opinions of others, including students, will help you better understand what is needed to accomplish mutually beneficial goals and objectives. Further education also allows you to develop new models that can be applied to yourself and others.

Attending Fordham Graduate School of Education, I learned how to become a better educator and teacher. I've participated in principal leadership workshops and developed new curriculums moderating the performance of teachers as an administrative intern and professional.

I've had administrators and teachers, including principals, superintendents and prominent authors in the field of education speak to classes about how they have succeeded and measure success. Importantly, they've traced the paths through time that led them to where they are today. These paths are essential for providing models or 'mirrors' for others to learn to properly relate to themselves. Educators concur that answers often come from within, especially in the struggle to strive for higher meanings and values which takes the attitude and attributes associated with never giving up.

At the end of one particular workshop, I remember all of the participants again joining hands in a circle and the professor asking us to come up with one-word summations of the workshop in which we had just participated. The following were the responses from other teacher-participants: compassion, vision, leadership, humor, dedication, humility, love, joy, peace, truth, patience, understanding, insight, satisfaction, purpose, authenticity, discipline, power, vitality, conscientiousness, credibility, devotion, aspiration, mission, growth, wisdom, focus, performance, honesty, inquisitive, confidence, change, cultural, spiritual, balance, passion, perseverance, and kindness, among others.

Everyone at one point or another during their lifetime would like to aspire to the more powerful divine attributes. Eventually you can reach a higher level of appreciation along with genuine balance. It takes a little work and at first some chipping or chiseling away.

Adults have come to my fitness and martial arts schools throughout the years. Some continue to work with me on a one-to-one basis. Their true desire is to improve the overall quality of their lives. In so doing, they have learned about conditioning their bodies and understanding principles that can be of help to them now and for the future.

I have asked many why they were working with me and what they expected the outcome would be. Some students explained that they were looking for friends, some needed just to lose weight while others wanted to become more flexible, more focused, or needed to rid themselves of the stress and tension of their day. Some wanted to become more physically developed or gain weight, others wanted to become more spiritual. In all cases they were set to begin a journey that they felt would in some way improve the quality of their lives.

There were a variety of disciplines taught at my schools, including physical fitness and exercise, aerobics, karate, taekwondo, aikido, judo, ju jitsu, kung fu, tai chi, ninjitsu, yoga, self-defense, weight training, wrestling, as well as Thai and Western boxing. Most of the classes were taught separately but some disciplines were taught together. Each of the adults had long and short term goals and they developed their own programs. Some students believed that the exercise, meditation, discipline, concentration, and awareness that they attained from the different martial arts helped them overcome problems such as alcoholism, drugs, divorce, weight, emotional or mental disturbances, and gave them a more peaceful outlook on life. Many developed better ways of communicating their true feelings, establishing better relationships, acquiring greater self-esteem, and exuding confidence in daily living.

From time-to-time I lectured and here are some of the lessons that I brought to the class about a key principle for achieving true accomplishment, respect:

"The purpose of the bow is that you respect yourself and others."

"Humility is one of the greatest forms of respect, and respect makes relationships work."

"Respect means treating someone well, with concern, the way you hopefully would want to be treated."

"If you don't respect yourself you can't possibly respect others."

In Western culture, you probably won't be bowing to someone like you would at my school, so it is important to remember two reasons why you bow so that you can apply it to your life. Those reasons are respect and humility.

Humility is necessary for a healthy mind because it stimulates self-growth. You can't possibly grow spiritually or emotionally if you think about yourself with bravado, talk without purpose or reason, boast, or need to control everyone and every situation. These characteristics impede maturity and growth. To calm your mind and develop a strong body, you need quiet, relaxing moments that are youthful and innocent as well as devoid of undue self-interest. You need humility.

Leading the students forward to begin making more integral mind, body and spirit connections was more important than any other experiences at my school. The truth again is: Life is change and change is life. How and why my students made that change was of primary importance at the time, and still is.

Students often heard in classes that you must follow your path, listen to your heart and meditate on where you are now. We called this cycle wish, prayer and faith. This was a simple lesson to help students accomplish what they desired and better attune themselves.

I also always explained that the physical techniques of moving, kicking, blocking, punching, striking, and tumbling were only a small part of the class experience. The most important reason for training is to become mindful of the higher dimensions, higher attributes and stimulation of the mind and spirit which ultimately gives the body more strength and power.

Students often commented that their lives should have more purpose and I would respond by saying more knowledge is greater power. Inform your mind and body with positive straightforward insights and embarking on a journey with a mission to improve the overall quality of your life. This is one of the best ways I know of adding purpose, fulfillment and meaning to daily activities.

It is here that the first part of our adventure is complete. If you have followed along word-for-word, you have vicariously traveled through three decades, earned at least one graduate degree and would have decided that you were ready to teach others just some of what might be positively applicable from what you have learned.

Most importantly, if you become your own teacher, and apply just a handful of the insights presented, you will continue to move along at a post-graduate pace no matter what your educational background. You can learn the practices and techniques that will improve living in a substantial way.

Just as simply as you have traveled along the avenues of another individual's past, you can apply similar lessons and develop programs designed to begin at this point and stage in your own life. By opening yourself up to the learning experiences of others, you can not only apply those experiences to illuminate your life, but you have and can have the respect and humility to embrace new beginnings without preconceptions.

In other words, the life that you can chose to understand or leave behind, and the life that you can also choose to change, is really your own life. Where has your own life provided insights personal and precious to you along the way? How has it compared to the lives of others?

Once you re-group and re-ground yourself in the present based upon good lessons you may have learned in your own past, the lessons left to be learned are those to be learned as well as taught as new beginnings.

For a person who has stepped back as he or she should into a world based upon faith and true learning experiences from the past, new and often unique insights and experiences await. Now is the time to become that person who, today, needs only to rethink and then better understand how to recreate their own future. Aspire to the power and then learn the art that life itself teaches to those still willing to learn.

# Chapter Twelve

As an introduction to a more personal program, I would like to explain how students in my adult classes participated in a general physical fitness, martial arts and wellness curriculum. It will give you an overall picture of what the disciplines actually involve, as well as what can be accomplished through training. By adding diversity to the routines, the chance of becoming bored or not enjoying at least one segment of the underlying disciplines is greatly reduced, and the dropout rate from such programs is lowered.

Students would spend about a half-hour warming up if they were taking some form of martial arts, or one hour if they were taking an aerobic exercise. I didn't mind if students stayed for other classes as long as there was sufficient room.

Each classmate would bow and then come onto the mat. They would line up by rank, black belts to the left and white belts to the right. We would close our eyes for a few minutes. Together, we would begin with breathing exercises. Students were asked to remain in the present moment as long as their eyes were closed. Then, in an instant, we all opened our eyes, bowed and then proceeded with the warm-ups.

There wasn't much that classmates practiced without having participation and facilitation from me directly. I always worked out and trained diligently in each class with the students in addition to my own personal workout schedule. Their own warm-ups consisted of stretches and limbering exercises. Warm-up combinations were changed from class-to-class.

The word discipline came up often. Everyone was expected to do the best that they could. Each time we would try a little harder and that would ensure that progress was made individually and that experience would bring us closer to accomplishment. When people are given positive reinforcement they try harder and put more zest into what they are doing.

For instance, if you can't touch your toes now, then keep trying and eventually you will get closer to touching them. Just remind yourself that you are getting closer each time and you will.

At one point we would all stand in a straddle position and try to do splits. I made certain that no one rushed or tried too hard because if they did, not only would it become awkward, but also they could get injured. Everyone took their time and stretched a little bit more each day and in time they were almost all able to do a split.

There are no quick answers or remedies for learning since it truly is a lifelong process. Discipline, hard work, time, and patience will eventually give you the rewards that you are seeking. Just enjoy the exercises and good experiences and remain positive during each successive moment.

Following stretching we would do abdominal exercises and push-ups. Many students doubted themselves from time to time but I explained that it's like jumping in the swimming pool or getting behind the steering wheel of a car. Eventually, it becomes more natural.

As simple as these basic exercises and routines seem, they can become quite complex. How many of us practice these formats when we awake in the morning, after an afternoon break or at work? We follow so many other routines that our lives inform our systems to accomplish, such as taking the bus to work, eating sushi or a superb quiche for lunch or driving home at 5:30 p.m.

After accomplishing basic exercises over-and-over and simply trying the best each time, through simple repetition you would not believe the positive outcome. My students were actually amazed that with proper training eventually they could do a spinning back kick or a handstand. There isn't much that you can't do if you just keep trying each day.

Living life well is an art. Like art, you can start from beginning points, add creativity with a sense of discipline and then display, exhibit or re-create nearly anything: a mood, series of actions, still life, way of approaching others, painting, collage, sculpture, song, spreadsheet, database, symphony, dance, or whatever your particular life's art form suggests. You have a beginning, and then another section or situation becomes completed, and then you keep adding layers of art or chip away at reality, or fantasy, similar to work in sculpture, until you are satisfied with the final product or result.

It's the same in life. The more you discipline yourself, or focus on what you are doing and what your goals and aspirations might be, taking just one step at a time, the easier it is to accomplish objectives. It often starts with the most rudimentary of applications. The key thought here is to have a beginning. Or, new beginning if necessary. And then maintain a focused sense of continuation.

Our class would begin with fifteen to twenty minutes of cardiovascular exercises to get the heart rate up. We either accomplished this by jumping or jogging around the mat. We also practiced basic kicks, punches, blocks, and strikes.

After practicing these, we would increase the speed, accuracy, alertness, and focus of the same exercises. The movements became intense, more intricate and sometimes fierce. In general, everyone was working hard on their stamina, concentration, balance, strength, will, and in the process all were getting a powerful workout.

There were parents who would bring their children for instruction and end up staying throughout the session. I remember one parent, Bob Cavaluzzi, who would bring his two children Andrew and Todd, and practice stretches in the back during the sessions.

I would always explain to the class, "Think about how you could apply some of these basic principles of stances, form, agility, and focus on other aspects of your life. Single out the situations in life where you feel your life could have more purpose and meaning and then apply similar exercise formulas to real life situations."

Can you picture the exercises thus far as we have described them for the class? See if you can focus on just one or a set of several that you might enjoy mastering. Envision yourself practicing that exercise until you have it down as well as you think you need. Envisioning is half the battle. The second half is to begin to do the exercises until you have mastered them close enough to the satisfaction of your vision. Of course no one should begin any exercise routine without the approval of their primary care physician or a related specialist. Remember, a medical practitioner can always help establish a new physiological vision and mission along with you.

Now that you have imagined mastering the art, how would you apply it to life? Think of a situation in life where you feel deficit or would just like to witness improvement. Imagine being able to practice bettering that situation through physical release such as prayer, meditation, exercise, jogging, sports, blocking and kicks, better balance, or running in place. Now try to figure out how you can work on a given situation applying relative methods to make it better, alone or with the help of others. Think of that situation as you step it through its logical steps or stages to completion with satisfaction. You've then accomplished your positive goals with respect to that particular situation.

Do you understand how you can clarify a circumstance or sets of circumstances by physically or mentally applying a remedy or series of positive initiatives and then methodically pursuing a successful outcome? All that's left is to actually accomplish the objective, just like you physically accomplish exercises, that is, one sure step at a time. It really is just that simple.

As we have been able to change our moods by momentarily tapping our subconscious which can hold distinct alternatives, we can also set up a solution to almost any problem in life. By applying determination and perseverance to create a positive outcome we will accomplish a final positive objective. It begins with mind over matter and the rest becomes a manner of form. Just as it does in any form of life art, creating or re-creating one piece of the artistic puzzle, exercise or human challenge at a time.

Through exercise and discussion, I would ask the class to think how they could arrive at a higher plateau in life and accomplish a simple balance on that plateau in a way that they could live daily and interact with others. I encouraged my students continuously to achieve a sense of belonging and a willingness to become a higher being. This means a person with greater values, goals, purposes, and a desire to follow their own truer nature in life.

Imagine for a moment that same goal for yourself: to elevate your psyche and attune yourself to a higher set of qualities and values, whatever that might mean to you. Then, to apply at least some of that knowledge to yourself, another person or other people in general. It might be an increased sense of religion that enables or inspires you to help an elderly relative, developing a greater sense of concern for a problem child or furthering your own understanding of the power of prayer or transcendental meditation. Whatever 'higher value' means to you today, it can become even more meaningful to you for tomorrow.

As we attain our more profound goals and objectives in life, life becomes simpler and uncluttered. With purposeful accomplishments aligned, we become more balanced and in tune with ourselves as well as the pacing and practice of others. It is truly amazing how just simple challenges, targeted to right not wrong behavioral patterns, can change almost any circumstance, attitude or situation we would like to see changed in time. All we need is the imagination, willpower, practice, patience, and perseverance. Suddenly the art of living becomes an integral part of our hopes, dreams and personal as well as professional experience.

# Robert Cavaluzzi, Jr.
## Former English Teacher, Spring Valley High School

*When I think of Ted Smith, I think how Ted has made me feel 'unstuck' in my life. When Ted says we're going to meet somewhere, sometime, some place, I take that with a grain of salt because time is relative with Ted. He has helped me deal with something that used to structure my life. But time is timeless for Ted. When Ted changes his appointment or does come but on an unexpected date or time, it doesn't matter. The important thing is that he is here.*

*In essence what he has really taught me is to live in the moment. I have read all the Zen masters and studied the Zen Buddhist texts but Ted has helped me to put their writing to the test. He has shown me the importance of living in the moment and how time is meaningless.*

*He has not only helped me to understand the Zen concepts that I had read but he has also helped me to understand the principle of 'non-pursuit' in its practical application. In other words, he has shown me that the more I strive to pursue an object or a person, the farther away it, he or she gets. I've since learned to allow things to happen, to cast the stone, to watch the ripples and see where they bring me.*

*Before my divorce which was certainly a turning point in my life twelve years ago, I was a friend of Ted's and he was my friend. But, our true test of friendship was during my time of crisis, during my divorce when I would simply get on the phone and ramble on to him about all my frustrations and angers and fears. Maybe he was there on the other end of the telephone, maybe he wasn't, but he showed me the importance of 'letting go.' And, he became my master, which brings me to how I met Ted.*

*He was the karate teacher for my sons Todd and Andrew who are now twenty-eight and twenty-two. In my searching for a yoga teacher, Ted was the teacher in one of the classes that I sat in on. I knew immediately that he was the person I would want to be the karate master for my sons.*

*While Ted was teaching my sons the katas, I would be meditating and doing yoga stretches. I learned at that time at least one of the things I was able to know almost intuitively, that it was important for my sons to have their space, and for me not to infringe on their space.*

*I never learned a single kata. I never practiced a single move of karate because my sons never asked me to join them. This was their arena and I was intuitively intelligent enough to allow them to pursue it. Coincidentally, it allowed me time to pursue my own yoga and meditation and attain peace and self-confidence. I left with the same peace and self-confidence that they left with. Ted's class became the center for that.*

*Another thing I experienced and realized through Ted was that there is no such thing as 'chance;' that people come into my life and events occurred that I never asked for. But, if I could reach a state of awareness where I could allow them to happen and follow them, it would be, in the final analysis, for my betterment and aid in my development.*

*I said initially that I met Ted in pursuing a karate master, a teacher for my children, but I really met Ted without realizing it through his father. His father owned a realty company, Mel Smith Real Estate. I purchased a home for the nanny for my children when they were born. She stayed on and she was supposed to live in the house that I had bought. When she decided the neighborhood was not nice enough for her to live in,*

*I ended up having to rent out the house.*

*I go back to this because that house was what got me involved in real estate investment and what has sustained me through what could have been a disastrous financial period after my divorce. The houses I later decided to buy using Ted's father to rent the apartments, and then talking with Ted's father helped me to learn about real estate that encouraged me to take real estate courses. I never realized that Mel and Ted were related when I was doing my karate search.*

*It was not chance or coincidence. All that was connected then, all of it is connected right to this very moment: those investment properties, the meeting with Mel Smith, the meeting of Ted, Ted's companionship during my divorce, and my friendship with Ted ever since.*

*Ted showed me another thing: In making someone else happy, I was making myself happy. He showed me that the more that you give of yourself the more you receive. There was a certain peace that Ted showed me. There is no time or reason or place that is absolute for Ted and I needed to learn that fluidness. I needed that flexibility. I needed to learn that flexibility in my life and needed to be reminded of it.*

*Ted taught me not to sit in judgment of people who choose that life. It was not a life that I would have chosen, and today I still probably have not chosen it. I have moments of timelessness, of unplanned activity and certainly my goal is to live in the moment. But, when I wake up in the morning, I still write down my list of things I have to do, and another list for things I want to do.*

*Society taught me the list of things I have to do. It's what I lived by in my years of teaching and it's what has helped me enjoy my retirement for the last two years because now my list of things I have to do is centered around what I want to do. They are not part of a job; they are not things I'm paid to do. The things I want to do are the fun things that have no time limit or boundaries, or schedules. They are things that are spontaneous even though I may write them down.*

*All the Zen Buddhist texts, yoga, meditation techniques at the ashram - - all that theory Ted has shown me to practice serve as a constant reminder as to how I choose to live my life. Ted has taught me the true way to love. It occurs whenever I make any appointment with Ted; it's a test of my flexibility, a test of my non-judgmental attitude that I'm trying to nurture. Really, each time it becomes a test of my love.*

*I enjoy watching him because now it's a non-judgmental gaze. And he tests that every moment, much as my children do. Todd who is now twenty eight and a very successful corporate attorney in Washington D.C., and Andrew successful owner and manager of a health club in New Jersey, each of them test my beliefs and values constantly, and look at them and I see the strength and independence that they have gained through the karate discipline that they learned from Ted under my non-judgmental gaze.*

*I would like to believe that the strength that they receive from the influences like Ted Smith and his karate classes have made them out to be the loving, compassionate, kind, good natured, happy individuals that they are. They are not carbon copies of me. Nor do I expect them to be. They are their own persons and to a great extent Ted Smith helped me understand the person that I am and that gave me the confidence to allow my children to be the people they are meant to be.*

*Certainly no one book is the answer. I have learned through Ted that it's in people and engagement with people that the true living of life exists. Therein lays 'The Power and Art of Living'*

*Teddy Smith and Bob Cavaluzzi*

*Bob Cavaluzzi and Teddy Smith*

# Chapter Thirteen

In an exercise class that embraces the martial arts, following a cardiovascular workout everyone should practice 'katas.' This is formal exercise and at the heart of karate training. Each kata is representative of a dance-like movement that resembles movements of animals. There are many katas, some with one movement and others with hundreds or thousands of sequences. Katas are very much integrated with body movement and motion and are interconnected with dance.

Katas are an art form. When students practice they practice katas with grace, determination and spirit. They put their heart into each step and each detailed move.

Katas are also the inner dimensions and representations of a person's ability to practice a dance or a story. The way in which a story develops is much like the way a kata unfolds, with a beginning, purpose and an end. What you do along the way as you practice each specific set of movements is an indication of your ability to exhibit and grow physically, mentally and spiritually. When you practice each kata with precision and sincerity it shows. Katas improve your balance, your concentration, your endurance, your attention span, and your strength. Kata practice strengthens the areas in life where there are weaknesses. If done with clarity and in good spirit katas can improve your physical wellbeing as well as make you understand more clearly. They also help you relax and reduce stress as you practice.

Kata training develops a truthful spirit and the progress that you can make in a life force that seems insurmountable. If your life is confused and filled with conflict I would suggest that you practice katas.

Katas also provide an excellent aerobic exercise. The daily practice of kata as a physical exercise improves overall health, coordination, stamina, tempo, concentration, and movement. Effectively, it can improve the way you act toward others as well as give you a balanced more positive attitude when dealing with other people. It keeps you alert and your reflexes are able to react more adeptly, mentally or physically.

If life is truly an art then we must learn the art forms necessary to achieve harmony. Overall quality of life improves as our lives become more harmonious. To accomplish specific gains in our daily lives we need to embrace specific disciplines.

As we shared our important life philosophies together in high school, college and graduate school, we balanced education with fun. We learned with environment and graduated with an openness to continue to learn. Together we understood that respect and humility played vital roles in awakening us to new positive experiences and that physical exercise can strengthen the mind, body, spirit, and soul. Applying mental exercises, not unlike physical practice, to circumstances and situations can challenge us to effectively change those very circumstances and situations. In doing so we can create better harmony in ourselves as well as those around us, improving daily living and overall quality of life.

We have now a bridge to the future that needs to be traversed. That bridge, kata in all its meanings, needs to be fully understood and applied. This is a bridge between our own inertia, or simple mental envisioning of what we can change in our lives, and the actuality of becoming empowered to initiate change. That change represents empowerment physically, emotionally, mentally, and spiritually. I believe that this empowerment begins with the practice of physical disciplines that can eventually accomplish true mind, body and spirit connection. Beginning with the desire to establish this connection together, we can begin an intelligent and well-calculated journey. That journey can then take us to the higher values and attributes where methods for living life as an art become more apparent. Eventually, spirit and soul evolve in tandem with the rest of our natural growth.

In establishing kata sets for ourselves to learn and grow together we can challenge all our strengths and strengthen all our weaknesses. In so doing, we will find the places within ourselves where problems actually dwell and not need to apply unnecessary external remedies to resolve inner conflicts. As we grow, learn, cleanse, and strengthen ourselves, these problems will disappear as a result of our exercises.

With each new kata comes a new set of challenges. With each set of challenges we find a new set of remedies to negate unpleasant internal and external circumstances as well as situations. Inherently, we will resolve those circumstances and situations and when we decide, apply our new remedies, steps of practice or katas, to succeed.

Physically, we first need stretching. Then, we need aerobics and following we need traditional exercises to help build cardiovascular strength. Finally, we can begin with the art of katas.

It takes great dedication to do a kata well. In class many students didn't realize that all of the hidden moves from the katas can be used for protection. The intricate movements can be applied to any grab attack or counter-attack. If an individual can succeed in these alternative measures there is no doubt he or she could apply them to other forms of negative situations or circumstances when they arise.

All the moves are contained within the katas. It just goes back to the basics. In kata it's movement. In life movement or proper continuation is combined with basic life principles: truth, integrity, self-determination, contentment, respect, obedience, rectitude, love, and compassion. You don't always see life's purpose for yourself and those you love because it evolves. However, this is similar to not seeing a physical opponent who creeps up from behind. You may not understand or comprehend an ultimate purpose or true nature in life until you are faced with difficulties, which may involve suffering or tragedy to awaken the inner self. But, self-determination before the fact can help avoid these pitfalls that too often befall the unaware, sometimes even successfully deterring tragedy or loss.

Awareness doesn't come when everything remains status quo. No change comes without challenge or a purposeful new direction. When you try to change something or someone else you need to have the tools available to properly choose and then implement. To dedicate one's self to change, steadily and productively, one needs to set a course that will first accomplish innermost goals and objectives. Learning the physical, emotional and mental techniques needed before, not after the fact, one develops practical patterns or katas to successfully accomplish present and future change.

Life's ultimate principles are certainly not easy to understand but they are attainable when your heart, mind, spirit, and soul become pure and selfless. This is accomplished through innocence, faith and seeking proper knowledge and truth. Eventually, universality falls into place, hopefully as both a human as well as divine perspective. You can do it. Anyone can. The value of a healthy life is immeasurable. The ability to learn and share that higher level of health and wellbeing takes practice and remains an art.

When you become true to yourself your real nature shines through. When you become true and right for others the spiritual powers of life are further unleashed and transformed into mutual benefit. Right action will occur and you as well as others will find a comfortable place in the grander scheme. You'll smile more, enjoy life more and eventually appreciate how precious it all really is.

Learning the disciplines of physical fitness, exercise, kata, and the martial arts teaches you the better postures for daily living and positions you for advancement as well as defense. Katas can be the pivotal point in the beginning of this new experience.

With my adult students we progress from self-defense to sparring. Most of the people I've trained have attempted fighting with another student to practice their experiences. The faces and expressions that I've seen in competition over the years are innumerable.

Back in the old school no one wore pads. They fought bare fisted and bare footed. The old training was tough: no backing away or not following through on techniques and responsibilities. Shouting was permitted and sometimes needed. Fear of injury was prevalent but could also precipitate injury.

Many feet can get elbowed by sparring partners. So, more and more students wore pads on their hands and feet, a mouth piece and other protectors.

Some of the matches were fierce. You could see the strategy and spirit that certain students placed in the match. They attempted to find an opening and then attacked when the other person's guard was down.

In life, when you drop your guard, you know what happens. You become a target, like a punching bag. You're often not aware or you have difficulty seeing clearly. To see clearly in life you must know who your friends are, understand your surroundings or environment and know what the most important things are that can make you feel whole. As important as sparring and competition with partners is for some, competition within one's self is an ultimate battle. The progress that you make is almost always up to you.

Students are encouraged to spar with anyone from any style or discipline. In this manner you can acquire knowledge from others and round out your own personal or professional perspectives and challenges.

Upon finishing several rounds of sparring, students took the weapons of the day off the wall. Sometimes we would learn about the 'bo,' a six foot stick that looks like a pole. A student once asked me what the purpose was of flipping a stick around your arms and legs. I replied, "It has to do with learning control. You are learning the bo for concentration, coordination and physical exercise."

When you hear the word weapon, you probably think of violence. However, farmers on Okinawa used these sticks as tools to graze the grass or dig up dirt. Traditionally the correct name for this particular apparatus is farm tool.

The class learned that weapons are extensions for hands and bodies. You can do a kata with a stick, sword or other instrument in your hand. You can also learn a dance with music and weapons. There are many proficient dancers that can use a sword or spear in a dance sequence. You develop a toned body and clarity in your techniques. It's like polishing silverware or riding a bicycle. It's also about cleansing your mind and spirit and working out your body in unison with tangibles.

If a sparring student dropped his guard he would be in trouble. Well, in life if you drop your guard or are not aware of your surroundings, your perspectives become unclear and you become both internally and externally vulnerable. If you're not in touch with who you are, where you are and why you are there, then you need to reconnect. When you understand that it's also about patience, perseverance and balance, then you will succeed.

Prayer or meditation is not just a passive activity conducted with your eyes closed to achieve inner understanding, peace and harmony. Students have told me that they have developed greater awareness and insights about themselves and their practices from the concentration that preliminary mental or spiritual conditioning reinforces. That initial and then continuing concentration forces a form of meditation that can be positive and integral for success.

Cool-down is another form of concentrated expression. The class lines up and sits as the sweat pours off their faces. They do a few slow breathing exercises, attempting to regulate breathing patterns. This helps everyone feel calmer and in tune.

Sometimes the students also try a few yoga postures. Many enjoy these postures and appreciate great improvement over time. They eventually exhibit great posture with great body movement and graceful stances.

"Establish your center, your balance within, and then close your eyes." Our actual meditation could last anywhere from five to fifteen minutes, depending on the situation or need. Students would open their eyes and look straight ahead. They would rise slowly and conclude with a tai chi set, something also taught during class. Sometimes we move slowly through about fifty steps and you can see how the external part of the workout becomes balanced with the slow and very peaceful transitions of tai chi chuan.

If you try just the right contemplative meditation at home for five to ten minutes per day it will give you an edge on positive activity. You will develop more energy and understand better what should really attract your attention and focus during daily activities.

You will also be challenged by an inner voice. It should explain that you shouldn't have to focus on trivial issues because you are replacing bad behavioral patterns with focus and meditation as a good behavioral pattern in itself. Your inner voice will automatically guide you towards an exact moment and meditation will help keep you in the present. Don't worry about the past or the future, not if you can well-manage the present. It takes time, energy and focus to stay centered and get to a point of being alive comfortably in a present moment. However it's then that we become well-poised for future opportunity.

It is here that I would like to more appreciably develop the use of kata as an exercise in daily living. By associating its particular form to the art of painting, one can more readily envision the contiguous lines, patterns or ultimate expressions kata can enliven. If you hold the paint brush and stroke it unto a canvas, you can devise your own systematic approach in terms of beginning, middle and end. Then there is the even deeper significance within the contours of the painting process which sometimes becomes the abstract. Finally, there is the representation of expression itself. In this sense alone, katas can be utilized in a myriad of circumstances and ways to affect a calculated or even spontaneous result in life.

Other ways that you can relate to kata are in sports. That's what can parallel kata in the martial arts. It is why all such arts eventually add up to the art of living well in the real world.

A physical education teacher can look at each sport and find a kata connected to it. For example, each sport has a set of rudimentary skills. Each sport also has their own set of drills associated with those skills. If the moves or skills have a pattern, an arranged set of movements, or have a set number of plays, those skills or plays represent a kata or a line of movement within that particular sport.

If the steps or ways of moving a ball or executing a motion become important outside the game arena itself, then you have achieved something even more useful and powerful. You are now learning to translate good sportsmanship, good character, motivation, and discipline as a skill set applicable to life itself.

Explaining this to adult students from the outset would help them recognize the value of applying the translation of skill set processes to their daily lives to effect positive outcomes. It's not only what you do or learn that counts, but how you can intelligently transfer applicable principles and skills to your life to keep it balanced, organized, caring, and fun. I consistently emphasized during classes that getting a great physical workout is important for overall health. But, applying the principles of character development to life is also an ongoing practice of self-perfection, benefiting your own wellbeing as well as that of others.

One student once asked, "How can you possibly perfect yourself?" My answer was, "By working on human weaknesses that block you from understanding clearly and honestly living in a truthful way. This means being honest with yourself and with others."

Self-perfection is unattainable but one can strive to come close. Even when you make mistakes in life you can learn something from those mistakes and avoid making the same mistakes again. If you recognize and learn from your flaws, then through prayer, faith, being kind, gaining knowledge, proper application of katas or correct sets of experiences, you will finally develop keener insights, heal and prosper. Importantly, you will become better inspired to help others learn, live and love better as human beings, themselves.

# Chapter Fourteen

Many of my students benefited from more far-reaching aspects of our program. Many individuals did indeed gain self-confidence, respect, improved their concentration, and achieved further self-esteem and awareness. Some of the students displayed the willingness and developed the obedience necessary to listen and learn. In so doing they learned to balance what is important in their lives against what is superficial or meaningless. They were also able to make these distinctions more clearly.

What can be said about several students in particular was that their strength of character was a tremendous factor contributing to their ability to communicate honestly with peers and fellow workers. This not only encouraged their own development but supported the group as a whole.

The nature and elements of character development are essential in the building of physical, emotional and mental stability. It is here that we enjoy the benefits of righteous words and concepts such as: truth, sincerity, respect, courtesy, humility, love, joy, compassion, kindness, rectitude, fortitude, grace, prayer, faith, and hope. Many of these words can become positive mantras or focal points of reference in our lives.

These words also have significant meaning in the way that they can be applied and practiced. Aspiring to higher moral principles and practices as well as actualizing them on a daily basis may seem utopian, ideal or just a fairy tale. Not so. For many it is a lifelong challenge and test to attain that higher level of spirituality that goes beyond a world that is finite and imperfect.

You may be able to appreciate spirituality internally but find it hard to practice externally. However, with perseverance you will one day be able to properly reach outside of yourself and help someone else through life's changes and challenges. Hoping, praying and acting in a way that will awaken the heart of another and re-inform their lives helps you experience a higher level of spirituality yourself. You will be further infused and reinforced with added powers that will now have both practical and applicable values. This, in itself, gives life more meaning.

I have also received much positive feedback from others in the past in these same areas of self-awareness, sharing and growth. Some have explained they have learned to apply moral principles to their daily lives, transferring the knowledge that they gained during our sessions through special practice on their own. In the real life experiences that they have explained, and the way many have intelligently re-confronted problems that they have encountered, I know that they will also gain further inner strength and eventually succeed in assisting others when the right time comes.

As stated earlier, 'life is change and change is life.' You need to learn and grow from the changes that affect you personally and professionally from moment-to-moment. Only then can you find the reasons and true meanings of why life itself is expanding or contracting in your own situation. Changes can rectify the present, help you learn and eventually make you stronger. You can become better able to make informed decisions that will positively affect your life and that of those around you. Just remember, one step or decision at a time.

Reading works of good value is very important. Positive theories that you learn from a book or a story can often be applied to real life situations. You should be able to make yourself a more wholesome person from what you read. By applying what you learn to practice you can become more resilient and positive in nature, cognizant of your comparable strengths and weaknesses. Hopefully, you will become more humble and compassionate toward others because of the lessons learned from good reading materials.

If you have good health, you have nearly everything. How much money do you really need to survive? It might not be able to buy good health but can sometimes assist with better health or the time and assistance to accomplish healthier outlooks and practices. However, if you can assist those who are in need of help through charity you will strengthen not only your own spirit but might also help improve the health and well-being of another, and of course, society at large. Also try to remember that it's never just about you. Being 'I-centered' and egocentric is too easy in today's 'instant gratification' world. Suddenly you'll find that you have external problems but lack the internal objective resources to properly respond to those situations.

There is always good energy and bad energy traveling in and out of life. How do you discern the differences between the two? When you're in a right situation your true nature will respond to it. If you're in a bad space or wrong situation your innate positive self should tell you and you will rebel.

You can always internalize or rationalize good or bad and right from wrong. If you internalize, an inner 'sixth sense' should let you understand what the right alternative can be. However, if you rationalize, your inner 'bad self' will set you on the wrong course. It's being able to discern the correct path that can help you determine the right state of mind and learn how to correctly discern the subtle differences between positive and negative energy forces.

Sitting quietly and praying or meditating on a positive life force will help you choose the right decisions to make. Remember, the foundation for all answers lies within you at all times. That is soul. The soul really does have right answers to life and especially your own life's course. The closer you get to its true nature and especially Divine Creator, the better positioned you will be to attain the graces, understand and apply the wisdom learn from any question life presents. Strength, character and good spirit ensue. It is not always just a simple solution or practice that effects change. That is why tapping and unleashing the true power behind change is not just a practice but an art.

What does character have to do with it all? Having integrity and good character develops inner strength and good spirit and will make you see in a more simplistic manner. Developing good moral values, respect for one's self as well as others and the ability to seek truth as a spiritually enlightening way of life can only turn change into beneficial growth. Importantly, mind, body, spirit, and soul will become unified in a common cause for internal and external benefit.

All at once, social situations, physical surroundings, the higher qualities at work in the world, and any new circumstance that you might encounter in life will become more identifiable, especially in terms of good and evil. Good will always overcome evil. So, it really becomes a simple matter of good practice enabling us to eventually overcome the limits of time.

Adult students should strive to make senses sharper and more alert. With that particular goal in mind you can always remain confident that not only are you learning from each other but also becoming more aware of the differences between positive and negative energy forces.

Real life experiences are one of the greatest sources of learning. However, we should never lose sight of the importance of our own attitudes toward situations. These attitudes can very positively or negatively influence our real life decisions. It is the application of knowledge with the fuller understanding and practice of higher virtues that can better develop one's self as well as help prosper humankind.

Did you ever know someone who had the greatest knowledge of books, trivia, politics, history, literature, and more, but didn't have one ounce of common sense? In a world of specialization this becomes more-and-more a frequent occurrence. Worse, is an adult with very full knowledge in any or several given areas or fields of interest yet lacking morality or a proper frame of spiritual reference. It is too common, wrongful and too incomplete.

The ability for adults to communicate with each other was always recognizable in sports and martial arts class and the students' curiosity to learn was remarkable. Some could kick better than others, others punched better and some blocked stronger. One performed a snappier and flashier kata, while another student performed a slower more graceful form. One student could be strong as a fighter but the next student could have a neater more polished technique. Each one had a different level of potential achievement in a select area which could be ascertained by testing interests and bounds in different aspects of a given martial art. And, you could always recognize the student whose attitude toward situations and challenges was improving along with self-esteem and the ability to 'give back.'

Everything reverts to the basic elements of attitude, behavior, character, ability, agility, and grace. Never lose site of your basic or inner nature because it's your true nature and it holds the answers to your true self. Through the practice of basics you can better appreciate your life as well as the simplicity in challenge and the innate ability to create positive change. Practicing basics takes away distractions so that you can think clearly. It also puts you in tune with truer beginnings. Remember, new beginnings at any stage or place in life are very important and indeed, necessary for growth.

If your motives for learning basic techniques are genuine and forthright you can eventually conquer many areas that are in need of improvement in your life. You can always learn humility by starting at the beginning. The need to understand first and know who you are or who you are not along the way will be attained through patience and right action. Once you have gained the knowledge necessary to discern your own life's purpose, you can then begin to truly understand others, their motives and gains. This in turn re-informs your own initiative to become more perfect in a too often imperfect world.

Do you remember the purpose of our original look into the mirror and travel back in time? It was to help remove the clutter and put ourselves back in touch with what our original goals and ambitions were. Then, to decide whether they might not still be the right paths for us to pursue, develop or explore.

What were your own original desires and aspirations in life? Perhaps some of your initial learning bases were not as broad, fulfilling, stimulating, or nurtured properly by professors, parents, other students, or friends. Or, perhaps you never had the opportunity to become formally educated and decided or needed at one point to just work and learn by endeavor and through experience. If so, then now is the time to become young again and think of reapplying a correct developmental process.

Let's no longer learn from the experiences of an adult. We should now begin a journey of basics and begin to learn through the eyes of the smartest people in the world, our children. Within the minds of children dwells right knowledge and truth. Through the lives of children the hopes and promises of the future are fulfilled.

# Chapter Fifteen

I arrived at the United Nations After-school Program over ten years ago. During the past years I've worked closely with children from all backgrounds and ways of life. It's been quite a unique experience and has actually refined my own abilities, especially as a teacher.

Multicultural is a word that references openness and the ability to work harmoniously with an extraordinarily diverse group of individuals. At the United Nations program, it meant a very bright group of children of diplomats and workers from around the world.

Teaching and learning with children is both stimulating and challenging. As a teacher you can inspire children and bring out the best in them as they grow physically, emotionally and mentally. My role was to nurture their abilities specifically in physical fitness, sports and the martial arts and as others did in dance, art and academic subjects.

One can always teach children about more significant values such as kindness. One can also go beyond daily lessons to a peaceful and meaningful experience where you tap into their young innate qualities. Herein rests a tremendous resource that I have learned as a result of educational experience. Learning from children can be magical as well as truly existential. It can also have life-long meaning for oneself.

Children need attention just as adults do. Children also have an honest mind, clean of many temptations, greed and trickery. But, never underestimate the aptitude or ability of a child. You can never buy true respect from children but you can work hard to earn it. It's obvious that it's not only about instruction but moral character and principle. Isn't right from wrong one of the first things you try to teach a child?

Then, understanding the need to strengthen your own character with similar reinforcement, especially as adults in an adult world, is a good thing to begin today.

A true inner nature means a normal, natural, even childlike state. Greed, avarice, power, slander, selfishness, and exploitation aren't part of infancy. Rather, children and adults should be in the state of openness: to learn, to be kind, tender, loving, joyful, humorous, and sincere. In many ways, children start out from a perfect place of physical, emotional and mental wellbeing. Bringing out the best in each child is gratifying and each day brings with it a new experience. Bringing out the best in ourselves as newly formed children should be equally as rewarding.

Not one group of children is the same as another. Each child has special higher qualities, needs and desires. Every day is a new program with fresh ideas. Spontaneity comes into play often because the mood of a younger aged class can change quickly and you have to be ready to make subtle adjustments. You have to think quickly, from meeting school buses to preparing a snack for the children, from talking to a parent to bathroom and water fountain duty. Managing students' homework is also a lesson you need to learn quickly as a teacher to be able to assist in diverse coursework.

If a child needs help with their homework you work with them. If they are crying they need to be comforted. If they are laughing because something is really funny, then you laugh with them. If they start pushing each other around then you separate them.

If one child is making fun of another child you sit him or her down, find out the facts and then have one apologize to the other as appropriate. Without some sense of discipline and respect for others you don't have a class. This methodology applies to the school as well as to home environments. Parental supervision and control is necessary at all stages of child development.

As an adult in whatever job you hold in any field, without discipline and structure things will fall apart rapidly. You need a foundation, a sound beginning. You also have to show others that you say what you mean, mean what you say and then are able to follow through on what you say you are going to do.

Too often we forget the basic premises of character formation as adults in our personal and our professional lives. We can become falsely self-assured and forget that not only are we prone to mistakes outside of a well-disciplined and structured environment, but others around us are even more apt to slip if we set a bad example. Adults, like children, need a proper and supportive frame of reference in which to live, work and thrive, even if it needs to be self-imposed.

Our after-school program was divided into five areas: sports, fitness, martial arts, dance, and arts. In my specialty of physical fitness, sports and martial arts students were exposed to soccer, football, basketball, baseball, and track events. They practiced karate, tai chi, kung fu, yoga, and kick boxing. We also practiced aero boxing and cardio-karate for agility, as well as body dynamics and coordination skills. Children learn about movement and then how it can be applied to other areas of life as well.

You can see a great improvement in students' movements after repetitions of skills and techniques. When they get used to the stretching and it becomes easier you can recognize significant improvement.

For a proper adult program we would begin with the same areas of fitness, sports and martial arts. You will find that lessons that apply to children in these areas can apply to adults in the beginning stages of daily workouts. By creating a simple structure implemented successfully by pre-school children as a model, there is virtually no adult who is incapable of facing physical, emotional or mental challenges directly.

Children can progress well to martial arts, understanding basic principles, when they can relate well to programs tempered to youth. In such situations, and without adult preconceptions which can sometimes be a bit inhibiting, they are willing to begin basic step-through programs. Capturing the children pictorially at work in their physical exercise and martial arts training as we will show, one can immediately witness logical comparisons and parallels to adult training. The idea again is that beginning as children in any sense or at a starting point without preconceptions, we can build or re-build our lives in many ways, especially in areas of physicality.

Just like with the children, adult programs should be tailored to individuals and practiced one-on-one. Certainly they should first be approved medically. However, by following some of the basics outlined as we go along, from attitudes to elements, disciplines to structured routines, you will have a practical case to present to any medical professional and a point of reference for him to approve, accordingly.

# Dr. Stephen Scheidt, M.D.
# New York Hospital-Cornell

*There is no question that exercise is one of the coronary risk factors. Of course it is a negative risk factor; that is the risk factor is sedentary living or lack of exercise. We're not sure whether exercise is a primary protective factor or whether it operates through other coronary risk factors that is, regular exercise keeps people thinner, or keeps blood pressure low, or raises high density lipoprotein – HDL or good cholesterol.' The fact remains that more exercise is associated with less coronary disease.*

*One enormously important role of exercise is in limiting or preventing obesity. I think every thinking person knows that there is currently an epidemic of obesity in the United States. It's actually quite frightening to people who have to plan for the future. The number of overweight Americans is rising rapidly. The number of frankly obese Americans is rising rapidly. And the number of teenagers who are overweight, or obese, is very, very high. This will cause enormous trouble in the future.*

*What does exercise have to do with it? Well, yes Of course, you could stay thin by not eating. However, for most ordinary people keeping at a reasonable weight it is both a matter of watching one's diet and exercise. There have been scientific studies to show that it is remarkably difficult to maintain normal body weight without some routine exercise regimen.*

*The amount of time for physical exercise is an individual matter and I think the most important thing is not to push oneself at the beginning so that you get discouraged and stop exercising. It makes absolutely no difference if you start with light exercise five to ten minutes a day, and gradually increase both intensity and duration.*

*The way I start people who haven't exercised before is I tell them at lunch time to go out and walk around the block. Now if you walk all around a city block in Manhattan, you have walked four blocks. You do that for a week and then walk around the block twice. Now you are doing eight blocks; that's almost a half a mile.*

*Or, get a friend to do it with you. You don't have to walk fast and you don't have to push yourself; just do it and get in the habit. Now double it again and you're doing nearly a mile a day, or nearly twenty minutes of exercise a day, and if you do it every day, you've reached the recommendation of one hundred twenty minutes of exercise per week.*

When you ask about routine exercise programs and what we think is beneficial for cardiovascular health, most people feel that between thirty and sixty minute per day would be optimal. We recognize that not everyone can do it everyday. But, you actually lose the conditioning aspects if you let three days go by in between sessions, so twice a week is not enough. I usually tell people to aim for one hundred twenty minutes a week, that's either twenty minutes five to six times a week or thirty minutes four times a week or forty minutes three times a week. However, you really have to exercise at least every third day, otherwise you will get de-conditioned, your muscles will ache, you'll get out of breath, and you won't continue regularly.

I think that it is reasonably well accepted that physical exercise also makes you feel better. The speculation generally centers around endorphins, which are natural substances that are found in the brain and are released by physical exercise. There are substances that produce pleasurable emotions and physical exercise does indeed release these substances into the blood. Interestingly, the magazine 'Consumer Reports,' actually did an intriguing survey of its readers a few years ago and reported that the treadmill is the piece of exercise apparatus that most people stick with the longest. I can't give you any scientific explanation of why that is so.

I suspect that whatever exercise you are good at, whatever exercise makes you feel good, is probably the best exercise for you. I do recommend that people try out various types of exercise. A nice way to do that, by the way, is that if you're traveling and your hotel happens to have a gym, use it. Or, get a friend to bring you into his health club as a guest.

Try out all of the machines. I hesitate to give my personal opinion but I think that exercise bicycles and rowing machines don't get used a lot over the long term, and it's the good old treadmill that does. But, you don't need any machinery whatever to get you started unless you live in a very hilly area. Just go out and walk and then when you get better at it, jog.

Again, I recommend you find a friend, a spouse, or a significant other as an exercise 'buddy.' It's much better if you have somebody to do it with and also, you will feel shamed that you let the other person down if you don't do it on a day when you initially don't feel like it.

In general, exercise will reduce your blood pressure which reduces the risk of heart failure, reduces the risk of stroke, and there is now some evidence that it reduces the risk of Alzheimer's disease as you get older.

*Exercise reduces the risk of developing diabetes (or its severity if you already have diabetes) and diabetes is associated with all other diseases all over the body, but especially in the heart, kidneys and peripheral blood vessels (hardening of the arteries) everywhere.*

*Exercise almost certainly will strengthen your muscles, which is likely to mean less arthritis and less in the way of joint, ligament and other kinds of sprains or stresses as you get older. Physical exercise also reduces osteoporosis and the weakening of bones in the elderly that leads to loss of height, back problems and the broken bones that are so common in older people. If I had to tell you the biggest complaint of my eighty and eighty-five year olds who are still remarkably sharp mentally and whose hearts and internal organs are fine, having aches and pains: 'I need a new hip; or I need a new knee,' and this sort of thing, clearly if you are carrying around twenty or thirty extra pounds, you are going to have those problems with arthritis or osteoporosis, sooner.*

*As to relations between the heart and the mind or the mind and body in general, there are some things that might surprise you that are very well documented. For example, depression is a very powerful risk factor for heart disease and possibly for overall death rates. It isn't good to be depressed and most people feel that exercise is one good treatment for depression.*

*Another very powerful risk factor for heart disease, very much under-appreciated, is lack of social support: no friends! That's why going to a gym and interacting with the all the people at the health several hours, is a very fine thing. I'm something of an iconoclast on this but I actually think one of the main reasons why cardiac rehab programs (to which we refer patients after heart attacks or bypass surgery) work well, is because you go out and make new friends. You're depressed after you have had a heart attack, you realize that you are mortal and you have to stop smoking, you have to lose weight, you have to change your diet: all things you really weren't considering doing.*

*The tendency is to just sit around and mope, but your doctor refers you to the rehabilitation center and you go down there three times a week and you meet other people.*

*Social isolation is a very powerful risk factor for heart diseases and increases total deaths. The converse, having friends, is protective. Living with someone (you don't have to be married by the way just live with someone!) is protective and so is having a pet; although dogs, not cats. I'm* not so sure about this last, but there was at least scientific study published in a cardiologic journal stating that people with dogs actually do better after heart attacks.

It may be that you have to go out and walk the dog, so you have to get exercise. Furthermore, as any dog walker knows when you walk the dog, you meet other people. So, having a dog may work to counteract the social isolation factor and lack of social support. There is no one thing that causes a person to have a heart attack or absolutely protects one from having a heart attack. It's usually a number of things taken together, what scientists call 'multi-factorial' factors for coronary heart disease which includes high blood pressure, smoking, sedentary living, family history of early coronary, as well as some behavioral factors.

Depression is one chemical risk factor, social isolation a second. Anger is a trigger for occasional heart attacks, and there have been some very elegant studies done, including one that we were a part of at New York-Cornell. We interviewed people who just had a heart attack, finding out what they were doing at the time for twenty-four hours before the onset of the attack.

There are surprisingly few activities of daily life that trigger heart attacks, but there are a few. One of them, interestingly, is intense physical exercise in couch potatoes. We're not talking about usual exercise in somebody who exercises all the time, but the unusual shoveling snow during the first big snowfall of the winter in a person who hasn't had any exercise more strenuous than frequent trips to the refrigerator for the last several years. People who exercise routinely have a much lower risk.

A second trigger for heart attacks is intense anger for two hours after the episode of anger. We're not talking about just getting angry but about screaming anger, including throwing things, out of control banging the walls, or injuring yourself and others. Big time anger is a short term risk for a heart attack.

As to people who seem angry nearly all the time, or if you are the kind of person that flies off the handle every two hours, then you could increase your overall risk of heart attack enormously. In general, only a tiny portion of heart attacks is related to anger.

# Chapter Sixteen

Once a desire to excel and need for continuation has been established in a child or an adult it is amazing how quickly one can develop physically, emotionally and mentally. This takes proper application of correct skills and techniques. In particular you can often see the devotion and dedication that children have when they play a sport or practice a martial art. There is so much enthusiasm from youth after regular school hours. They have so much energy. Our place and duty is to channel that energy in children so that they become focused and productive. Why not so with adults?

The perseverance that children display when they are practicing their punches and kicks, keeping up high energy levels, is quite impressive. Watching them hit a hockey puck, kick a soccer ball, play another sport, or just throw a hard ball is fun. As their interest in sports develops their commitment during practice expands in tandem. And, their perspectives about what they are practicing become enhanced with motivational skills significantly improving over time. If they say that patience is a virtue then I'll add that both correct learning and proper leadership are also virtues. They are both fundamental for continuing success in life.

Not everyone learns at the same time or at the same pace. So, if a teacher once told you that you were slow or had a handicap learning, it shouldn't really matter. Or, maybe you did poorly on your SATs or achievement tests, but you succeeded by outsmarting all the preconceptions that other people might have of you in the work environment. Over-achieving isn't a bad thing when supported by moderation. But, how do past failures measure up in the face of present success? Scantily.

Everyone has different levels of learning and some can't learn certain things well at all. However, that doesn't mean that you are more or less intelligent or brighter than anyone else. Some of the students who you thought weren't achieving at a certain time are now achieving faster than the ones who received straight 'A's' on those multiple choice tests. Some students that were very quiet are now more extroverted than the students who did all the talking. Some of those slowly learning and introverted young friends that you may have found endearing are now adults who outpace their childhood counterparts in the real classroom called 'life.'

You should never pass judgment or second guess a child's or adult's intelligence or abilities. Each and every person has a special gift or set of gifts as well as one particular or group of talents. Some of the more recognizable talents are nurtured at an early age and others develop later when one begins to struggle with adulthood. Some don't even emerge until an adult is part of the mainstream workforce, or have had a chance to just stay at home dawdling with a paint brush, canvas or keyboard. You never know the true ability or personal needs of a child or adult until you remain open to the opportunity of enlightenment and proper communication.

A multitude of information can be garnered when you are receptive and simply paying attention. By listening you are learning about the child or other adult, and by communicating well with that individual you grow to know them as prospering human beings.

Do you have children of your own? Do you have sisters or brothers that have children or other exposure to children on a familiar basis? Do you take the time to discuss situations with them from their own points of view? Ask them about their lives and their opinions, their personal likes and dislikes, their hopes and their aspirations, and then just listen. If you take a little time to absorb the answers to these types of questions from a child, as an adult, you can better relate to those responses in the real world and challenges the child or you yourself might be facing. Then, when you re-connect with that younger person or your inner-self you can offer a new perspective akin to their own or your own true needs.

The art of teaching, and especially teaching children, gives the individual the desire and motivation to improve new skills and techniques. Some of those responses from a child or the child within you can take you by surprise. They can offer new insight or provide a new spin to existing circumstances. The better you understand yourself, your own experiences and the experiences of others the wiser and more diplomatically effective you will become.

Olympic Day at the United Nations After-school Program was very popular. At the end of the school year, we had the children perform their skills before peers, parents, teachers, and guests. It's exciting for them, the teachers and administrators as well as those who assist.

The children exhibit the skills they learned during the year by playing games of soccer, hockey or handball. They demonstrate baseball and basketball skills including passing routines. They have already learned the importance of respect for teammates, good sportsmanship as well as fair and friendly play. They have learned how techniques involving interaction are integral to success. These same techniques, including courtesy, are as important to everyday living as they are to playing sports.

All of these newly acquired attributes are displayed in one way or another during Olympic Day. Teachers as well as parents would understand first-hand how these good behaviors had or hadn't been applied to a child in the overall developmental process. This is not unlike the adult Olympics.

In professional Olympic Games, there are political, social as well as individual sportsmanship issues at stake all the while. Often, many of the internal issues are adjunct to the external issues, and 'win' or 'loose' becomes an even more universal end. This means that there is all the more reason to train with discipline, strategy and develop superior technique.

It's vital to be kind as well as firm, considerate as well as strong for your own benefit and the benefit of others during human developmental process. This includes sports, academia, work, and social activities. One's personal ambitions as well as goals and objectives can be substantially intertwined with any activity. This makes it fundamental to remember that in life it is never just win or lose. If it were, consequences along the way could often become too dramatic or dire.

Children, especially, need nurturing in an environment where energy is positive. You have to motivate and give children positive encouragement in the process of properly fulfilling their needs and aspirations. You also have to be concerned for their wellbeing at all times and for me, especially during sporting events, fitness and martial arts exercises and routines.

You can open a child's mind to creative movement, balance and flow by including sports, martial arts, dance, and art in their lives. This also fosters good communication skills for children, interaction with teachers and other good adult practices. These disciplines also provide an excellent introduction to socialization as children show pride and share their accomplishments.

After-school programs for younger children are readily moderated by parents, teachers or older students with proper guidance and professional supervision. Pre-existing as well as newer models are constantly in development and often wisely implemented.

In our program the groups were broken down into three. Group one was for kids ages four through six, group two was for children ages seven and eight and group three was usually for nine and ten years old. All three groups enjoy keeping fit and competing in sports. Their parents understand that it keeps their minds active and bodies energized.

The children watched exhibitions where groups of trained instructors used karate to break boards, demonstrate self-defense techniques and illustrate sparring katas in performance roles. The children enjoyed watching, learning and performing from adult demonstrations.

We also had students perform dances from various countries with music that exposed the children to various cultural backgrounds. We incorporated martial arts dance from Okinawa and Japan which gave the students a vision of combining dance with karate or other martial art skill sets.

In all cases curriculum models are developed with age, ability, cultural diversity, discipline, proficiency levels, and goals and objectives all drawn from adult programs. Adult programs in all martial arts disciplines begin with very similar models for performance.

As an educator with extensive teaching and practical experience in health, fitness and martial arts, it has not been too difficult to decide what would be best for children at the pre-school and elementary levels.

However, many of these activities are still uncharted territory, not so much for the age groups involved as for the combinations of exercise, fitness and martial arts programs. Together they create multifaceted achievements with related gains.

For instance, dance and martial arts complement one another. Our children are already exposed to various dances from throughout the world. We utilize African, Japanese, Spanish, and American Jazz. Students have also been taught martial arts from China, Okinawa, Korea, Japan, and America. If you look at the similarities between dance and martial arts you can understand the gracefulness, artfulness and strings of similar movements adeptly employed in alternate disciplines. Whether you are twisting, turning, jumping, leaping, standing, or sitting, you are in essence moving, and there are a number of movements that disciplines share.

It's amazing when students learn dance and martial arts simultaneously. You can see the motion of their bodies, the emotions on their faces and the creative way each student utilizes movement-to-movement form. They seem to learn instinctively how one art lends itself to another. Since our classes actually build upon each other, what is ultimately accomplished is both magical and mystical. In the end it becomes a higher form of balance and movement of mind, body and spirit. The underlying principles of spirituality inherent to the arts are also always at work and support the entire process.

This is where I feel the positive power to effect change enters in and raises the entire experience to the quality of life improvement realm. Without an underlying energy that separates ordinary practice from true experience there is no extraordinary gain or sustainability in practice. It is the combination of this special spiritual-like power with the art that elevates the process from ordinary routine.

At the same time, teaching as well as learning experiences are built, developed and sometimes revised as a new-formed practice. The resulting improvement represents a marked advance for the new learner and such advances usually translate into improvement in facets or pockets of learning for other educators. Obviously, sustained self-development incites specific as well as overall change. Hence, the quality of life is also positively impacted.

It is important to understand this concept from the outset because explaining about teaching children should have a direct impact on an adult. The idea is not only to relate experiences but also to challenge the adult individual to regroup and apply relative experience to their own lives. It is at this point that an individual should begin to develop sufficient background to implement underlying principles of development that begin first by understanding one's own 'child.'

With little or no exposure to the actual combinations of disciplines described, beginning as an adult and thinking like a child has significant benefits. Following basic exercises and better understanding the rudimentary steps needed for physical, mental, emotional, and spiritual gain is the essence of a formative adult program.

Similarly, as adults enjoy the experience of participating in competitive or alternative sports, they develop further athleticism and self-confidence. Competitive sports give us a chance to bask in the glory of victory or learn how to overcome the humiliation of defeat. Specific sports also help develop different agilities.

For instance, a hockey game provides us with greater overall conditioning, body skills and team motivation. Having a whiffle-ball baseball game gives one experience in coordinating bat and ball, field and players and running against a number of opposing factors and forces.

In field hockey while running and hitting the puck one uses practiced strategies including blocking to advance the puck down the field. This helps to develop agility in the face of direct opposition. Kicking the ball to the goal in soccer, blocking, trapping, and passing along the way, or most activities in football, all involve superior skills and techniques.

Track events build stamina and endurance which is always quite satisfying. These are reasons why jogging as well as running marathons can become popular personal pastimes.

Games that we take the time to play with children like "Simon Says," or "Red Light-Green Light," or even "Musical Chairs," help children to learn concentration skills and coordination. This increases attention span which leads to an overall ability to better perform. These physical and mentally challenging games when kept in proper balance with other activities all make children better able to succeed in school. How much more far-reaching are elevated level exercises able to condition an adult way of life.

Accomplishing feats in the martial arts, sports and dance helps children grow physically, mentally and emotionally. All of these disciplines take sincere practice and develop higher principles, skills and abilities. Martial arts and sports are also vital disciplines that in the end can calm a child's mind. Adults can always find the opportunity to reconnect to latent abilities and capabilities as well as develop more adept interaction with others in similar activities.

Art is also a peaceful but informative method of representation that can produce astoundingly enlightening results. Art improves one's creative energy as it develops focus and the visual exchange of ideas and concepts. It also develops physical facility for execution. People are always thinking and creating. You can often see in the final artistic accomplishment personal emotions and sensitivities coupled with talent that can add opportunity and potential through demonstration. It is no different in theory or practice for a child as it is for an adult.

Art also opens our eyes and spirits. Children as well as adults are able to relate movement of the pen, pencil, crayon, or brush in a particular drawing to particular circumstances, consciously or subconsciously. With the openness and ability to connect lines or objects into form or subject for either fun or interpretation one connects symbolic semblances of reality or imagination emanating from senses as well as interrelationship and experience.

As adults we spend much of our time simply connecting the daily dots that moderate or superimpose themselves on lives and routines. Imagine being able to flow through life as an artist with purpose and intent creating lines and forms on one's own volition instead of just connecting dots. You can create a better image, a better picture, and in effect, create a much more effusive and better day! Practicing art in all its multifaceted forms can one day earn us the opportunity to create a unique picture that can become the focal point or source for some or all of our tomorrows.

My karate sensei once told me that a true artist is an artist of life. To master life is to become an artist of life and master oneself. He said that truth, knowledge, perfecting human weaknesses, and becoming a better person eventually leads to that path.

I see this being accomplished when I watch children draw, paint or create objects such as ceramics. I understand that they are developing great hand-eye coordination skills, mental concentration and earning sincere positive reinforcement from their teachers. They are learning at an early age to develop their inner abilities and talents through personal expression.

Art is powerful, calming and a very special way of understanding or creating representation. An adult could spend a lifetime visiting museums and galleries and never run out of new thoughts that could make tomorrow a better place for everyone.

In addition to the United Nations Olympic Day during the last few years of the program we added a multicultural dance performance and art exhibition. This helped to fulfill the multidimensional purpose of the program, itself.

From an educator's and teacher's perspective, the United Nations program significantly influenced both my personal and professional life. I remember one of our first faculty meetings. The director of the program, Virginia, talked about the wonderful holiday performance scheduled for December and our roles in the event. I was to develop and direct the sports and martial arts; Thomas would choreograph the dance movements and teach dance routines; and Betsy would decorate the gym with drawings and ornaments. However, Virginia also emphasized the need for the children's homework to be accomplished on time and that we should rotate groups between art, dance, sports, physical fitness, and martial arts programs.

I have learned over the years how special Virginia has been in terms of both faculty and children. She always keeps a smile and positive attitude and greeted the parents with great respect. She directed and encouraged her faculty with much enthusiasm, admiration and especially, respect. She has also been able to channel her gentle but firm approach to help us develop better as teachers and leaders.

This is the nature of a good leader: to nurture, improve and respect. One can always learn from the experience of others and then apply it to their own human course. However, we are all born leaders and we should earn the opportunity in one way or another to help improve the lives of others.

The United Nations After-school Program was open to change, had new ideas and was always effective in bringing out the talents of children and teacher alike. It was in every instance able to find true potential while allowing educators and teachers the opportunity to develop their own abilities and teaching skills.

It's rare to find an institution with faculty that is not afraid to take educated risks, does not have favorites, is not political, and is willing to implement new ideas. Many other famous but more rigid institutions are often afraid or slow to adopt contemporary and evolving successful educational practices. We as individuals should all learn what it truly means to lead.

# Virginia Olney
## Director, United Nations After-school Program

*In the United Nations After-school Program, in addition to homework supervision, we offer activities in sports, martial arts, dance, and art. Here the children have the opportunity to express themselves in the areas of skill where they feel most comfortable. Getting training in these skills and participating in a certain amount of competition supports the process. We try to encourage positive competition and good sportsmanship, whatever the activity.*

*We demand respect for our teachers. And, the children also have to feel respected. It's a two-way street. For example, in a real dance class no one talks back to the teachers because this gives the wrong message. Here at the United Nations After-school Program, we teach creative dance as well as some dance forms from other cultures depending upon the teacher's expertise and cultural background. In order to have the children accomplish anything in the way of skills, the class has to have a certain structure and a certain amount of discipline.*

*To be an effective teacher, one has to be disciplined, show respect and be kind whether it's a dance, sports or art class. This should carry over to how the children behave at home -- I would hope.*

*I think that it is very important for the children to feel good about themselves. Our children should be made to feel special and to be encouraged. I think that they get this through participation in the classes and activities we offer which are important to their overall development. Of course, we have a performance in dance each year, an art exhibit and sports days, which so many people support and attend. They are so enthusiastic about each of the activities and that the children have the opportunity to participate in the After-school Program.*

*The important thing is that the children feel adequate at the activities that they participate in here. It gives them a sense of accomplishment. On every level, the children need to feel accomplished in learning about the sports, art and dance. They learn to realize that there are other people around, particularly United Nations staff in the halls, streets and in the building, who the children should be aware and respectful of, not interrupting whatever they are trying to accomplish. Again, I would hope that when they leave here this awareness would carry into their lives outside the UN community.*

*In all the years that I have been teaching, which has been many at all different levels, from college age, down through high school, private school age children, and now as Director of this program for children ages five through eleven, I still feel that there is a great sense of hope when I see the children. Some of my greatest pleasures are seeing a child just so happy in whatever activity they are participating in here, smiling, with their eyes lighting up and observing their joy of movement.*

*We work with our New York University interns in the graduate dance program who help us teach creative dance, and help with whatever our staff needs them to assist us with. We are so impressed with these interns who also serve as good role models for the children. I think that it is very important for all of the teachers here to be good role models for the children and to encourage them, yet, at the same time, be firm, challenge and motivate them, be kind and understanding, and also sympathetic to their feelings.*

*It brings great satisfaction seeing the children's accomplishments, feeling that you are part of their development process and that you are a good influence in their growth. I feel pleasure when involved with the younger generation. It makes me feel a much greater part of our world. Universality is a good word for this. It makes me understand that I still have something valuable to offer the world.*

*It is very important to get the best possible people to teach these children. I just think of their smiling faces which is very inspiring. Just seeing their accomplishments makes it all worth while.*

*One of the things that also inspires me very much working in this environment at the United Nations is that the United Nations is home for the unification of all the various cultures, which gives a real global feeling. I personally think that you have to be aware of the world these days. You can't be just involved in your own country or state. You have to be aware of the world and of each other's cultures and the necessity of the diversity of cultures. You have to understand and respect all cultures and religions today. It's very important for us to accomplish and teach respect for the world and each other's traditions. I encourage our teachers to follow the principles set forth in the United Nations charter, of reaching out to children of every race, creed and culture.*

# Chapter Seventeen

It seems that the happier and more content teachers and other leaders are, the more they continue to develop and grow. And, the more we can all be affected in positive ways. We feel and benefit from the happiness and patience that teachers and other leaders exude. An atmosphere where there is objective freedom from personal frustration and professional encumbrances creates an environment more conducive to learning for children, young adults, adults, and other teachers and leaders as well.

Children are very intuitive and are quick to pick up on the mood of their physical and social environments. They can read you and determine what emotions you are experiencing even from the body language you display. Too often, we forget that adults are not really much more than grown children.

Adults often appear or act childlike in one way or another. Their attitudes and attributes can reflect or harbor childlike approaches to situations, events and other people. Inwardly, they may even have a very naive or uninformed impression of themselves that is also childlike.

We deal with these people and situations every day in our professional lives. Many of us confront these same childlike situations at home with our families. If we approach these circumstances as children as well, imparting a willingness to develop and grow more sensitive to the sensitivities of others, we can identify and better clarify situations as adults. When we approach these circumstances as adults objecting or prevaricating without thought and objectivity, we add to the problem instead of assisting or alleviating it.

A good teacher would know better than to impose negative adult formulas on children. Why some adults never learn to appeal to the child within other adults and add compassion or empathy for growth is just another example of adult sociological conditioning. Unfortunately, contributing to the unhappiness or not undoing undesirable childlike behaviors in adults only creates more sociological trauma. Many of these instances could be avoided with the proper application of psychology used to address a child's, not an adult's, nature.

Thomas, one of the instructors at the United Nations After-school Program, was a brilliant relating to adults as well as children as a dancer, performer and teacher. He always exuded a powerful yet sensitive personality. You could witness the juxtaposition of adult and childlike demeanors that were always used effectively in communication because he knew how to properly counterbalance them.

His dances were no-nonsense because he worked as an adult appealing to a child's more adult nature but never forgetting that each and every one was still a child. It seemed that there was nothing that Thomas couldn't do with children and often with adults. Whatever the children did Thomas was right out there with them, whether simply motivating or giving intelligent lessons in discipline and self-control. He could also get younger students quiet in less than a minute and was effective at all times expecting one hundred percent of their effort. He wouldn't settle for less, yet he could make the children laugh with his great personality.

Thomas' voice was clear, he was concise and you could always understand him. He taught the children to have respect for one another, develop a sense of determination, and certainly commanded respect from the faculty and children for this accomplishment. His multicultural dances affected the children's' lives in a positive way.

Thomas had a friend named James, "Obaya," who joined the program one semester. He wore white clothing all the time, smiled and had a great sense of humor, but he knew when to be stern if he had to be. He gave the children interesting classes in African Dance inspiring them to chant and sing native African songs.

Obaya assisted me over the years with sports and martial arts events. In return I helped him with his different dances and we incorporated his dances into our martial arts exhibitions. He brought a flow and joy into his classes and kids become confident in all of these areas of interest.

There are many things that I've learned from the After-school program about children and adults. Importantly, like children, adults need caring and attention. For younger people and adults to learn you have to give them your all, meaning that you must sincerely want to be there to help, and in a sense or way, become a part of their lives.

Adults are a very complex sociological group and deserve the same proper care and attention during the communication and exchange processes as children. What a pleasure it is to work with children and adults that are not only willing to become well-developed physically, emotionally and mentally but also aspire to the higher attributes, sharing the greater virtues daily with their peers. In the process children as well as adults learn to listen and pay close attention to the needs of others.

Too often as adults we approach each other with our own agendas, ignoring that they too have personal and professional goals and objectives. By putting others first you can truly learn and satisfy their needs. Consequentially, you better understand how to approach them with what you need if that should be the case.

Just like children, adults need to first understand and then be taught. In adult communication the process of putting others first is too often the exception not the rule. This is often why much adult communication fails. It is disturbing to think how much interaction between adults and children also fails for the same or similar reasons.

Most importantly, children like adults are always learning moral principles and virtues that will have affect the rest of their lives. It is a great feeling of accomplishment when students or adults come back years later and tell you what a positive impact that you have had on them.

I remember meeting the Secretary-General of the United Nations at the time, Kofi Annan, and his wife when they visited our program. I was teaching a fitness and aerobic class when they walked in with guards. I stopped everything for a moment and we all respectfully greeted them. It was a pleasure meeting a leading world figure and his wife who had a special affinity towards children. They each spoke to the children and I remember very clearly how they showed personal care, concern and respect.

Moral principles and humanistic values are important to nurture. When we develop as leaders it becomes more readily apparent whether or not we have succeeded. We expect our future leaders to have integrity, humility, respect, and obedience as well as exercise the higher qualities and values that can improve humankind. Yet, how many of our world's corporate or political leaders really practice these principles?

I am proud that our faculty at the United Nations After-school Program was able to nurture and develop the abilities and capabilities of our children to help them truly prosper. The children have benefited and will continue to grow. They have developed greater self-confidence through participation in the activities and have become more confident when they see that they can perform a skill and improve its qualities over time. They have also developed increased self-esteem when they feel appreciated and cared for by faculty and friends as well as in exhibitions and performances from the recognition and appreciation of others.

Boys and girls in our program began at a very young age to develop a high level of discipline, awareness, socialization, and team-making ambitions with decisions. Participation in our developmental program improved the children's social awareness as well as their communication skills for other children and adults.

The personal accomplishments some students have made through the years have been remarkable. Whenever we help to develop good character, good relationships and good behaviors with positive support and reinforcement in children, we as adults grow in leaps and bounds.

# UNITED NATIONS
# AFTER-SCHOOL PROGRAM

*Virginia Olney with Obaya-James Moore*

*Obaya James Moore (far left), Teddy Smith, Sylvia Fuhrman*
*Virginia Olney*

# Chapter Eighteen

As a teacher working with teenagers from various backgrounds and schools, I have found that high school students are a particularly challenging group. When I was in high school life was much simpler, however teenagers are still teenagers.

Teens need a good deal of attention. Unlike young children they are already well on their way to developing their own values and value systems. This needs monitoring.

Teens like to test the status quo and with it adults' patience, kindness, sincerity, motives, and intentions. They probe into your personal life and see if they can figure you out. If you are a free thinker and let them act within an atmosphere conducive to learning you already have made headway and have distracted some of their negative personal inquisitiveness.

Young adults always enjoy when you recognize them as special individuals. They appreciate your honesty and sincerity. As a teacher in any way, you have to keep lessons interesting. It is your chance to be creative and to perform just a bit. You have to help establish an environment they can buy in to, experiences they can relate to and hopefully a learning program that they will finally embrace.

Adults are really much the same in the learning and developmental processes. If you are able to follow along with some of the methods and examples that are taught to younger children you should already be aware of benefits that can be acquired as an adult. For example, if you become inquisitive and pick up a book or two on the martial arts for beginners, or at whatever stage you feel you might be ready to start or continue, you should have already gained from a contemporary child's development at a comparative stage as the children in the After-school Program.

It is at this stage of comparative development that you will confront a myriad of examples, and like a teenager, be a bit confused as to how and why you should proceed. This is fine because at this stage there is not yet enough professional background information to properly springboard. There are physical disciplines that need to be described, higher qualities and attributes that need to be learned, and, like teenagers at the middle of the adult developmental process, fine-tuning on the spiritual plateau. With these disciplines practiced and understood one can begin to comprehend what it is that really needs to be accomplished in the martial arts and ultimately, in life.

Let's travel a little further down the road before we begin to combine the elements of life that we have already learned. It will make it all a little easier in the end. There are a number of learning tools out there, and one in particular needs to be at least briefly explained.

Interestingly, one of the first schools that inspired me to keep teaching as well as continue to find new avenues in which to learn was Shaarei Torah of Rockland in upstate New York. It was a boys Yeshiva with Orthodox children from predominantly good stable families. These children especially enjoyed sports with football and basketball among the most popular.

I feel that the teenagers truly enjoyed my particular style of teaching. We would play basketball with rabbis praying in the back of the auditorium. Teaching an Oriental discipline like tai chi or meditation, which could have religious connotations attached, attracted attention from the school. I was allowed to teach these disciplines without including particular religious perspective. It was as simple as that.

Teenagers or middle learners like children learn at different paces. I try to treat teenagers as special dynamic individuals. The pace at which some events occur in education is similar to a cartoon: sometimes the action picks up to a frantic speed, sometimes it slows down. In the end it is really just a series of still life pictures unfolding at average speed. I think becoming a cartoon character at times is not so bad. You have a chance to laugh at it all, making the inane seem sane. Who was your favorite cartoon character growing up? Do you have one now?

After a while I became a teacher in New York City. The first school I worked at was located in East Harlem and was called Frederick Douglass Academy. It was a tough school but the new principal worked well with administrators, teachers and staff. It became a tie-and-jacket school, meaning that all the kids dressed up looking presentable each day. This was a wonderful lesson in self-discipline which for some was more difficult than others.

The principal felt that every inner city child deserved a quality education and a right chance in life: to communicate, excel and be loved like everyone else. The students also needed the opportunity to attend college.

Some of the graduates were accepted to very good colleges due at least in part to the encouragement of the teaching faculty and the benefit of scholarships. Many students developed the commitment and determination to succeed. The principal at the time was quite a leader who has since become well-recognized for her work at Frederick Douglass. She was always jovial and always exuded positive energy. Her good sense of humor helped to keep the day less stressful.

What can be learned from this is that you can turn a bad situation with poor conditions into something positive and constructive with the help of a good, competent and informed framework. No matter what the lesson is in life, if you truly reflect on it and understand it through the eyes of a child, teenager or neophyte of any age, you will experience learning without prejudice and in the most difficult and obscure of routines. The point is to remain challenged at all levels of experience.

You can learn much from the people you work with. There are certainly many different personalities out there. That's what makes work so special: the unique blend of people. When you apply their distinct directives or lessons to learning you can build and develop your own tailor-made program.

As you begin your own physical exercise and martial arts program make certain that you find a suitable method for development. Whether it be through books, video programs, exercise, martial arts classes, or personal training at home or at a gym, make certain that you remain challenged at all times and follow-through with the method. If you don't like the method, change it. If you're not stimulated by the instructor, find a new one. In the end it is you who are in control and you who need to take control. That's what it's all about.

Sometimes you're curious about what the other side of education is about, that is, administration. I've always been a leader rather than a follower and have liked being in the simultaneous roles of self as well as full-time employment. There are pros and cons to both situations.

We should never lose sight of the fact that most administrators were teachers at some point in their careers. Administrators should also always remember what it was like to be a teacher as well as a student. Being a successful educator means being both a successful teacher and a successful student. Learning never ceases, especially for educators.

This is a serious lesson to be applied to adulthood and especially to all areas of career development. We need to remain open to the challenges of youth, including our own, and new perspectives at work in our environments, especially as leaders.

When I worked out with the United States Military Academy wrestling team at West Point in New York I was particularly impressed with the coaches. They brought in great wrestlers and Olympic Champions. Different guests would come in to share their expertise with the team.

They were secure enough to have me come in and demonstrate teaching aikido and jujitsu to the wrestlers. I remember Coach Spates was a guest on one of my radio shows and had brought a guitar with him playing it live. One art can always complement another. It was fun being involved with the Military Academy because the coaches made the environment relaxed and conducive to learning as disciplined as it remained.

Once, near the neighborhood where I lived, I met a gentleman who was homeless. He would sleep in movie theaters and would panhandle at night. Eventually he became quite ill, his ankles became ulcerated. He didn't take drugs and wasn't an alcoholic. He was just a person who was unlucky and had become homeless. One day he was bleeding profusely and I knew that I had to do something. I knew that I needed to get him to a hospital and then help him find a real place to live.

You begin to wonder what goes wrong in other people's families or lives that could make them homeless, addicted to drugs or alcohol or anything else that is bad. Obviously you can't help everyone in life but you can try to make a difference for at least a few people, or just one at a time.

I'm fortunate to have come from a family where love, respect and support were the pillars of upbringing. I've always had guidance, interest, encouragement, and kindness from my parents. They gave me the strength, hope and courage to succeed. They were also a support for my development, inspiration and understanding.

When I grew up technology was not as important as it is today. It was easier then, less complicated and there was a more simplistic way of living. People sometimes say to me, "What has gone wrong with our youth, our kids today?" I say that it is the times that we are living in, the advanced technology, television, stereos, computers, DVDs, cable channels, Internet, chat rooms, and movies that are not always educational but violent. Parents are often not as directly responsible as they once were for their upbringing because of longer working hours and especially, more divorces.

It really is more complicated. And, when children begin telling their parents what they always want to do, we have major problems in the family. I wish the media would instill better values and ethics in the minds of both parents and children. I also wish that children could learn very early on that you can't have or always find instant gratification in life.

I explain to parents, if I can, that they need to spend more quality time with their children and be cognizant of their study habits. Setting up a plan with children and young adults that includes homework, physical activities, mental activities, proper rest, and review of the day spent can provide a home environment with learning structure that also shows familial character and concern.

Listen to your children. Listen to what they really have to say and explain to them what they really need in their lives.

Can everything that children do be monitored by the parent? Can parents establish moderation in the lives of their children? For instance in America youth are becoming more obese. Can parents spend more time with their children insuring that the foods bought and consumed have proper nutritional value? Adults should be able to politely say, "No!" to their children when toys or adult distractions take them away from their studies. In other words parents should be willing as much as possible to teach positive attributes and activities for future growth.

I could never tell anyone how to live their life. However, I could try to explain how I think one might be able to improve the quality of their life and that of others in the process. If you can take better control over your life as a parent, you'll be taking better control over your life as an adult. Having proper concern for your children and yourself is a good place to start developing truer values in general. Perhaps someday more of the media will arrive at this same important conclusion and make the messages that they deliver more constructive, acceptable and designed to help improve the quality and behavior in life for children as well as adults.

Children are special. You know that. So are you as adults. Be disciplined, firm and fair with children as well as yourselves. If you show and teach them good behaviors and follow through on what you mean then children will get your purposeful message. Provide a firm foundation for youth and adults and you just may find yourself with a useful new beginning in your own life as well.

*Physical Education Class, Beacon High School, New York;*
*front right, Teddy Smith*

*Teddy Smith demonstrating Aikido*

*Teddy Smith demonstrating Tai Chi*

# Chapter Nineteen

Multimedia is as at least as powerful as it seems and could be one of the best sources for espousing proper values. The development of Internet with its own special form of mass communication is just the beginning. It is also a tremendous reference for one to find information and in the process develop a realistic program for self-betterment.

Broadcasting in all forms can influence everything that we experience in life. As an on-air host in major radio markets, streaming live worldwide on the Internet, I have the opportunity to schedule many prominent guests and celebrities from professional fields. The intelligence and influence these individuals can have on life and lifestyle today is extraordinary. During live on-air broadcast interviews I have the opportunity to share with a greater public the significant aspects and attributes of their talents. The information gathered as research before interviews and the interviews themselves provide the most pertinent and insightful messages for growth and maturity in both personal and professional arenas. Another's life opportunities and challenges can very well be transferred if one remains open-minded to other appropriate patterns that can create positive impact and offer proper change or fine-tuning of direction.

From past broadcasting experience in a number of smaller markets I've come to appreciate many different ways of life including musical tastes. I have also met many interesting leaders in their fields representing diverse cultures and communities. However, working from my youth in New York City proved to be most informative because I learned quickly to appreciate the tastes that a large listener audience required.

Along the way I have met as well as worked with a number of great programmers of our time. Having a hand in programming or at least sharing opinions with those responsible for broadcast content from the start created its own career pattern for me to learn and follow.

Later, I was involved with night shows booking prominent guests. It was amazing to learn how many celebrity interviewers and guests supported campaigns for feeding the hungry and accomplishing other extraordinary work with prominent charities.

What is important about broadcasting is that you can and often do affect other people's lives in a positive way. There are so many media personalities who do just that.

What was neat about work at WPLJ was that it was on the same floor as WABC Music Radio 77. It was easy to walk down the hallway and wait until the light was out on the door to walk into Studio B where Dan Ingram or Ron Lundy hosted on the air.

Dan Ingram was a pleasure to watch at work. You could see how meticulous and precise he was and he would make people laugh with his quick jokes between the music and jingles. He was a true professional and so was Ron Lundy who had a particularly friendly warm voice and style.

Following these wonderful experiences I worked with the famous Joe Franklin. There can never be another Joe Franklin. His unique qualities captured the hearts then, and still do now, of some of the most famous celebrities of our time. I worked as a talk show host and DJ on a variety of stations from WTBQ Radio in Orange County, New Jersey, to WJUX Radio in New York and also New Jersey. Work and friendship with him continues to inspire my on-air broadcasts.

Frank Truatt, the owner of WTBQ, is another source of inspiration in the media world. He always has a friendly easygoing manner. His programs are insightful and informative and programming 'state of the art.' Danny Stiles, a great announcer for radio stations WNYC and WNSW, once explained that he liked the way I sounded and to keep up the good work. He was always a concerned gentleman but was never afraid to tell you what was on his mind, good or bad.

When I worked at WPAT Radio in New York City as a DJ and talk show host a particular on-air personality, Zev Brenner, was instrumental in helping to develop my career. At the time we were part of the evolving leased programming phenomena that was consolidating radio broadcasting throughout America and working with an Orthodox Jewish community.

When they presented me with sister station WNSW to also be an on-air talk show host we interviewed celebrity guests such as film star Christopher Reeve shortly before his death, Andy Rooney from "Sixty Minutes," Sam Donaldson from ABC News, Mary Tyler Moore, former Mayor Edward Koch, Harry Jessel, who was then Editor-in-Chief of "Broadcasting and Cable Magazine," Joe Franklin, Sid Bernstein, Lally Weymouth from the "Washington Post," and countless other celebrity guests. We discussed every topic imaginable and always from an objective and informed perspective.

Why do I explain all this? Because radio is a unique entertainment media that provides pertinent information, education and for its participants, including the show host, a great sense of leadership. Importantly, it provides a challenging opportunity to remain objective which to me is of utmost importance in all aspects of life.

Radio is stimulating and creative. It's a changing profession where you have to keep pace and you need to be ready for adaptation or quick revision. That's the nature of the business, to keep working how and where you can and just work as well as you can no matter.

Individuals in every walk of life have the same opportunity to meet other individuals who have complementary authority or knowledge in the same or another field. It often takes very little to gain access to the professionals whose assistance or guidance can support, encourage and develop your own professional goals and ambitions. Challenging better communication not only broadens one's horizons, it can also provide access to new and more challenging initiatives.

Life is filled with opportunities just as people themselves are. It is simply a matter of understanding and then communicating one's own hopes and desires properly to others. Just like listening to a child, someone can and will listen to you and take your ideas and perspective seriously if only you as well try to understand.

All of my work on radio has assisted other professional endeavors. These endeavors when taken as a whole have created the educator, teacher and student that I remain today. Each has improved my career as a physical fitness, sports and martial arts instructor.

Your own endeavors can become part of a life program that not only becomes well-rounded, but also better informed in each and every area where you intend to excel. By developing your own life programs and then seeking the knowledge or assistance you might need to properly learn and grow, you greatly enhance the quality of your own life as well as the quality of the lives around you.

*Teddy Smith and Dan Ingram*

# Joe Franklin
## TV and Radio Personality

*Well Teddy it's a pleasure to be chatting with you on this momentous occasion and I would venture to say that I've gotten much of my inspiration and motivation over the years from those that I've interviewed. My first guest ever was Eddie Cantor, the famous comedian, who said to me, 'It's nice to be important; but it's more important to be nice.' So, I try to be nice. I never flaunt any fable. I have nothing to flaunt. I'll just say what Bing Crosby said, 'I'm just an average guy that sings a little bit.' And, I was lucky to be around at the right time when television was lighting up on the daytime.*

*I did what I thought was the first pure, organic from-the-bones talk show; a little bit defiant, but not in an overly aggressive, assertive or nasty way. This is what you do with the nasty people: Kill them with kindness. Let them think that they are putting one over on you. It's just a question of keeping a happy attitude in life and just having it in your bones, in your blood and in your body.*

*Just keep up your own frame: no nasty streak, no vindictiveness, no getting even seeking, no revenge. I've been double-crossed and triple-crossed and hurt by the best. I've known people in that position. They throw darts at the picture of the person who betrayed them. They hate them; they despise; they curse. Well, I just take my licking and I just walk away. The best revenge is to deny that person the pleasure of your company. And, the best way of annoying them is by ignoring them.*

*Well, Teddy, it's just a question of common sense. Of course, common sense is not that common these days. Many people today are insecure. There is a reason for everything. The key words today are 'insecurity' and 'fear,' which after a while leads to depression. The depression rate today is staggering and it's a matter of self-ego and self-esteem.*

*I try to tell others when they are depressed that things can get worse; and they usually do get worse. What you need to dip into is have belief in one's self. I'm not going to be corny and say smile though the April showers, and just know that times are not the best right now.*

*The homeless rate is staggering; the divorce rate is staggering. Three married men have said to me that things are so bad on the outside that they went home to their wives. It's just a matter of things being tight right now.*

*I love to help people, Teddy, and one thing is that I expect nothing in return; because you never really get it anyway. And, that is called gratitude. You need big binoculars to find gratitude.*

*Just remember, people tell me that I gave the first big exposure to Barbra Streisand, to Woody Allen, to Al Pacino, to Dustin Hoffman, to Bruce Springsteen, to Eddie Murphy, and twelve more people like that, even Michael Jackson. Julia Roberts used to sit in my office and answer my phones. They always ask, 'Joe do they come back and say thanks?' Well Teddy, with the possibility of Bill Cosby and Tony Orlando, most of them don't come back. Because I symbolize and represent and signify times when some of them, whoever they were, were broke and down-and-out and people don't want to remember those times. Maybe it's shallow; but it's human nature.*

*They see me and they say 'Oh there's Joe Franklin,' and they walk across the street and run. You see they don't want to be reminded of the times when they were broke and I had to give them carfare to come to the studio. I mean they were so broke, that someone else would resent it. I don't resent it though.*

*I don't look for any thanks or gratitude because you can't really expect it. If you get it, it's a pleasure. It's unusual and it's much appreciated. But, you generally don't get the respect and the thanks that you would like to in life.*

*Remember Teddy, don't get even with anyone: no vindictiveness, no revenge, no filling you body with poison and acid and hate. Just swallow it all and walk away quietly and let them wonder why you've had no desire to get even with them. You know that irritates people more than getting even with them.*

*In this business called show business, instead of being scattered and turned down in life and being rejected applying for jobs, pick one, or two or three people and hound them. It's a question Teddy of the word called 'perseverance,' and not taking no for an answer. And, don't let it get you down, no matter what.*

*There comes a time when you throw in the sponge if you can't make your desired goal a reality. Then choose something else. Because, eventually with time, you get back to what you originally had in mind. Remember don't let it get you down if you don't meet your standards the first time around. Keep trying.*

*It goes back to once again facing rejection, facing hurt, swallowing pain, and then moving on. If someone puts me down, not knowing that I may be on the phone extension listening, well someone else might get upset and offended and walk away in tears. But when I hear someone badmouthing me and putting me down, I only feel sorry for the other person. It is so immature, insincere and insecure about his or her self. So he or she has to let it out by criticizing somebody else. Deep down they are really very jealous.*

*The point I'm trying to make is don't let it all bring you down. Just pity the guy who says something bad about you and again, don't look to get even.*

*I would like to say that this book, 'The Power and Art of Living' is required reading for those in search of happiness and satisfaction in life and it does exist. This kind of a book has a conscience and as a guide, it's a must. It's a must read.*

*Joe Franklin*

*Teddy Smith and Joe Franklin*

*Teddy Smith and Bob O'Brien, WPAT Radio, New York*

*: Mike Ellenbogen, John Luke and Bob O'Brien*

*Bob Cruz and Dave Kreiswirth,*
*WABC Music Radio, New York*

*Above, second from left, Andy Liu; third from left, Jenny*
*Lacsmana; fourth from left, Danny Stiles; seventh from left, Teddy*
*Smith; below, second from left, Arthur Liu; third from left, Chuck*
*Leonard, WNSW Radio, New York*

# Chapter Twenty

Adults can help others become stimulated by positive energy, kindness and the will to succeed. Focusing on positive stories and energies and learning attributes like patience, courtesy, compassion, respect, and humility will assist greatly in the developmental process.

With an easygoing approach to mental and physical balance and a special sense of awareness we can seek to keep others happy and content as we interact with them daily. We can actually impart a wealth of knowledge and a great learning environment to others continuously by just being open to another's way of life.

Children, young adults and adults all have an inherent interest for learning and a great capacity for understanding. They certainly learn better when the atmosphere is positive and proactive. All people have the ability to learn something new each and every day of their lives.

Creating an environment of internal and external peace and tranquility for ourselves and others should be a goal for each and every one of us. By exposing ourselves to different types of positive influences we can always learn something new, especially to enhance the mind, body and spirit connection which is fundamental to any overall development program.

The idea is to try to find what is important and to have quality time so that you can maintain clarity in thinking and surroundings. We all need time to sit back and relax. Then we can slowly begin to realize what exactly we are doing and be able to get a better grip on what our priorities should be.

We also need to stay focused and centered. If we can begin to attempt this wholeheartedly then we can learn and grow without clutter or baggage. We should strive for a perspective and concern for humanity by realizing that help and concern for people will also bring our own vision to the better place it is meant to be.

Instead of placing thoughts and desires too often on 'I,' we can reach higher natural and spiritual plateaus by emphasizing 'you' and 'they.' We should remove many of the 'I-ego-selfish' thinking patterns from our lives and replace them with good thoughts and good works for ourselves and neighbor. As we have seen before, spirituality brings empowerment and empowerment, self-improvement. The art of living is supported by power and creates improvement in the quality of life for ourselves and others.

Of course it all begins with a genuine, realistic and humble concern for one's self. This is much different than selfishness or self-aggrandizement. And what can be worse yet, always advancing one's own agenda. If we can rid ourselves of one-sided motives and begin to think how our initiatives can be applied for the benefit of ourselves with at least respect for other others we add a second more challenging dimension to the program. Our lives become purer in terms of both motivation and activity. Separately and together we can all find the higher meaning and purpose for our existence. Indeed, we have been put on this earth for that very special reason.

Almost everyone asks him or herself in life in one way or another, "Why am I here?" "Is life a test?" "How much can I take?" "What do I have to give?" "What is there to give back?" "What is ever enough?"

Have you ever helped another human being find the truth? It is a wonderful experience and it becomes a truly compassionate and everlastingly memory. You can learn significantly from this experience both internally and externally. And, that is the point. Doing good for others brings self-improvement into our own lives one way or another and all of us closer to the truth.

There are so many great lessons in life that can be learned each and every day through contemplation, prayer and guidance from beyond. Eventually we will find our own faithful and true answers also within a truly universal perspective. As we do, sharing becomes another great lesson to learn.

Some of the most significant sages, prophets and masters in life had certain intrinsic attributes in common. Each had first come to realize that their lives were in so many ways finite. Many also suffered, surrendered and let go, eventually living in a very special frame of reference on a truly spiritual plateau.

They also knew that much of life was mystical and much of reality could not be seen through the human 'eye.' They realized that it takes patience, rectitude and divine presence through prayer, faith, contemplation, and grace to truly see and really understand. They would also come to a point of self-realization knowing that life is a lesson broken into many parts, often not at first understandable by finite minds. However, at this point, divine insight, intuition, wisdom, and enlightenment entered in and assisted.

Through struggle with these and other relevant matters, sages, prophets and masters eventually find solace and peace. Through right metaphysical understanding, righteousness and goodness there is always peace. Even when we stray from our spiritual needs we have better learned how to put ourselves back on the right path to make our lives more meaningful and complete. This is an inherent power and subtle art of living.

It is through higher knowledge that the masters of aesthetic disciplines shared their totality with students and ultimately many with all humankind. Many began and continued as we should, as children on the physical plateau working though emotional, mental and spiritual commitment to realize right and righteous human adulthood.

If we begin to understand that we have been placed on earth for a reason, this becomes a reality check for many of our subsequent actions. Life and the reasons for life are always meant to remain somewhat of a mystery. So is death. If we remember that life, similar to the earth on which we grow and prosper, is always in motion, transition and continuation, we can begin to unravel that mystery with all of its attributes, answers and consequences. This is in itself a significant reason for existence.

There are so many other purposes for life, many of which make us strong in different ways. If you haven't had that much inner strength before then perhaps you haven't spent enough time reflecting on the more important values in life. Even if you recognize that you have made mistakes along the way, and we all have, try to reflect on those mistakes. After admitting shortcomings we can better understand ways to improve the nature and quality of our lives and again, of others.

What is really wrong in our personal existence? Is it a character defect, a drinking or drug problem, an illness, the bad results of an accident? Are you learning to walk or use your arms again or have you just learned about correctly improving your own physiology?

Maybe you were once homeless or close to homelessness, going through an unpleasant divorce, angry at family members, or maybe there was a recent significant death around you. You might even be in the process of breaking up a romance or failing an important educational course. As diverse as these situations may be, or potentially become, you need to come to proper terms with the situation before making the right decision as to how to move on. Starting in the present and stepping through a problem one careful move at a time can help you avoid making mistakes for the future, some that you may have to live with for the rest of your life.

How can you become a more compassionate stronger person that can benefit from the negative aspects or bad obstacles that have interfered with your life? You should always be able to turn a negative experience into something positive and eventually, into a higher level lesson for learning. I and very many other professionals in varying ways of life believe it can be done. It may take patience and perseverance but working on and within yourself can be challenging and quite rewarding. Forget the frustrations, anger, obstacles, and road blocks and apply correct discipline to move forward and become a better person. Each time we accept that we are not yet perfect, and that human imperfection is everywhere, we have created another 'new beginning.'

If you are tired of living in a certain area because people haven't been nice to you and choose to relocate your residence as a result, remember you will find a new set of people who may be kind or unkind, good or evil someplace else. Just be prepared. Hopefully they'll be a better group and more suitable to your temperament. People are a constant and consistent challenge and always invite you to find out more about yourself and themselves in one way or another. They can also invite you to change for positive reasons.

How much can you take? It can eventually come down to how much you want to take but should include what you can learn from it all. Herein, it becomes a matter of patience, reflection, endurance, and growth.

Certain people may have been brought to you for a certain good reason, as coincidental as it might seem. The point is that once you have contemplated any or all necessary circumstances you are already on the path to enlightenment. And, enlightenment becomes fulfillment. To me spiritual awakening is always a burst of dawn for an individual.

The purpose of all this is again physical, emotional, mental, and spiritual growth as well as stability. If this can all be accomplished simultaneously, all the better. But, remember, no element of human nature can significantly mature without another.

How can you process all of it and become wiser, kinder, more compassionate, more understanding, elevated, and truthful? First, be honest with yourself and others and you will begin to find yourself more insightful, more intuitive, more desirable, and more spiritual. The more goodness that you place in your life the more good energy will come to you. Ultimately, this will affect your entire being, deepen the dimensions of your soul and bring you to levels of existence far beyond imagination.

Our physical, emotional, mental, and ultimately spiritual journey is also a constant journey into the psyche. Weaknesses and strengths eventually come to light.

Don't try to apply the reference of time to your journey because spiritual essence doesn't necessarily work in a dimension of time. Life, spirit, soul, and love are infinite. Through self-improvement, prayer and faith the entire human condition, weaknesses and all, can yield to strength. Character imperfections are simply places where the true Spirit has yet to thrive. Applying the right aspects, attributes, grace, and righteous characteristics invites Him to dwell within and without forever.

# Chapter Twenty-one

## Exercise and Fitness Programs

This first point is to understand the need to exercise to improve fitness and achieve wellbeing. If you are out of shape and working towards better physical condition, or in shape and thinking about what you can do to increase your stamina, endurance, awareness, and flexibility, daily exercise is the key. Many individuals train and some even cross-train. I encourage people to exercise every day, whether it's on your own, in a class, on a team, in a club, or in a league sport. There are many benefits to overall health achieved just by proper exercise and developing a total fitness plan for wellbeing.

Everyone today has a different idea about working out. I believe in a professional plan that is practiced consistently and followed through as diligently as possible. A program that will enhance the quality of your workout should exercise your entire body.

It's always important to stretch first before doing any cardiovascular exercise. You can sit for about fifteen minutes and stretch out your legs by reaching for your toes with both hands. You also need to be warmed-up and ready before impact exercises. Individuals will develop pain from high impact exercises without proper stretching over a period of time. You really need to take the time to stretch. This should be a minimum of fifteen minutes but a half-hour would be better.

Make your exercises constant and consistent, meaning that you do the same group of exercises each day without fail and really try to be patient with yourself, concentrating as you go along. It is better to do one exercise properly than five without being diligent. Work quality rather than quantity is always a higher virtue.

The added flexibility you will find in yourself after just a few months will also be considerable. Proper stretches will work all the muscles in your body and you will feel more limber and agile. Once you are, you are ready to begin cardiovascular exercises.

When you read different exercise and fitness books you will find that they offer differing information as to time elements involved in a workout program. Some say one-half hour, others suggest an hour or others an hour and twenty minutes. The truth is each of us has a specific level of tolerance for workout. Here, moderation is the key. Just enough is fine but too much is overkill and dangerous. Too much can also cause burnout. One should stay on a program once it has been medically approved and hopefully, periodically supervised by physical checkups as well.

It could take anywhere from fifteen minutes to a half hour to work up a heart rate. Everyone's metabolism is a little different and we are all built in different ways, which also impacts results. Normally, your heart rate when you are doing aerobics, running, taking martial arts class, or playing a sport, will exceed one hundred beats per minute. You know your body best. See how you feel as your heart rate rises. If you feel tired or fatigued, stop. And remember, stretching everyday is important.

Cardiovascular exercise should be done at least three times per week. If you are training for a specific sport, martial art, aerobic, or fitness activity, the program can change depending on your specific needs and goals. The object is that you keep pace on a daily basis so that you can maintain a personal sense of discipline as well as an ultimate sense of satisfaction, accomplishment and stamina. Whether your intention is to lower your cholesterol, lose weight, build strength, or just feel better about yourself, it is healthy to set goals and even healthier to accomplish them. The most important point, key to overall fitness and wellbeing, is that you stay consistently active.

Working out is not only good for your heart but it will also boost your energy level. This should help you cope with the pressures of everyday living and the stress that comes from daily activity. If you can find the time to exercise between fifteen and thirty minutes each day consistently, then you are getting places. If you have learned tai-chi, yoga or any martial art, you could add another fifteen minutes to your fitness program by incorporating that discipline following your cardiovascular program. If you really have time, try some weight training every other day. But make certain to work each muscle group alternately. In the end, don't worry about the time, just keep exercising.

Jogging is an activity that I diligently engage in every day. If you manage to do your cardio workout each day for fifteen to twenty minutes you can replace it every other day with a fifteen to twenty minute slow jog. You can build up the intensity and time as you go along.

Follow an approved program as diligently as you can. In addition to fitness exercises, if you have interests other than workouts: tennis, golf, basketball, soccer, volleyball, hockey, even engaging in an assortment of martial arts -- karate, taekwondo or kick boxing, all of these can develop great endurance and strength. Yoga, tai chi, Pilates, aerobics, and tae-bo are also exceptional workouts to try and hopefully continue.

No matter what specific fitness program you are taking, following the points outlined should give you a versatile alternative approach to fitness. They all have elements from standard conditioning exercise that will enhance more formalized practice. These are at least an addition and always an alternative because they incorporate a number of primary disciplines that can positively impact fitness, health and overall wellbeing.

After building a more structured approach to fitness both physically and mentally one can construct a parallel program with martial arts, simply from a new beginning if you haven't challenged yourself in this way before. Many of the approaches later defined are areas within the martial arts that you can pick or choose to start routines as well as add or progress as the case may be. However, a firm grasp of personal history and contemporary ethics and culture as they already affect your daily life is needed before embracing, structuring or re-structuring these complementary programs.

# Chapter Twenty-two

## Meditation

There comes a time during your daily routines when you need relaxation and some sort of calming meditation. You need time when you are not distracted to sit quietly. Try this in the early morning for ten to fifteen minutes and then again in the evening for up to fifteen minutes. Calming your mind and relaxing your body will keep you balanced, introspective and content.

You don't have to try to do anything, you just need to sit and follow your thoughts. Your own mind will guide the process. You don't even need to strictly follow contemporary meditation practices or other practices with or without religious connotation. My program of relaxation and meditation has little to do with religion. It has to do with improvement and tranquility in your entire body.

As long as you're in a calm state of mind and your actions for practicing are sincerely motivated by peace, your overall attitude will improve. Each aspect of your total reality can become clearer and so can your thoughts, overall internal state of mind and your personal relationship to the physical in general, that is, outward surroundings.

Meditation helps you better differentiate between what is considered real and what is really an illusion. To make the proper distinction between reality and illusion is to also understand yourself well. Proper relaxation and breathing techniques can assist in both sitting and standing meditations.

To be in a space and place of total reality, one needs to know how the five senses: smell, taste, feel, hearing, and seeing affect the natural state. This can be accomplished through meditation, which is also just another form of self-reflection. Meditation teaches you about the great importance of spiritual balance and relaxation and how you can calm your body, ridding it of stress and sometimes even physical, emotional or mental illness.

First, sit quietly in your room or a place that is comfortable to you. Take one deep breath in and exhale slowly. Bring your palms together and then breathe in. Raise your arms in the air and keep your palms together as you slowly breathe in and out. Try this three times. Then, close your eyes and breathe normally.

Everything should begin to become more centered and focused. If you don't have to worry about an appointment, time or other commitment, then open your eyes only when you feel a sense of relaxation, tranquility and peace.

Stand up and cross your hands so that the palm of your left hand rests gently on the palm of your right hand. Take a deep breath and let it out. Now, breathe in and out for three cycles. Close your eyes in the standing position, bend your knees, have good posture, and look straight ahead. When you start feeling at ease and centered, open your eyes. You have just completed a beginning meditation and relaxation exercise.

Congratulations! Meditation is a very powerful means for accomplishing personal goals and achieving overall increased stamina, self-improvement and success.

# Chapter Twenty-three

## Prayer

Prayer exists in most faiths and perhaps in one way or another in all. First, it is important to realize that we as individuals don't control most of the things that happen in the world, never mind the unknown universe. People are finite. Even life in its own way can be considered finite. Afterlife is eternal.

We need a purpose in life, with direction and structure. In order to achieve a higher purpose you need to first find the living force, power and grace at the hands of a higher authority. Prayer is a bridge between the human or finite and the infinite. To many, prayer is adoration, petition or thanksgiving to God, who is recognized in the monotheistic sense as the Supreme Being.

Your prayer should consist of asking for spiritual guidance as well as physical direction in life. Ask for forgiveness first, and offer prayers for those who have wronged you. This is an effective way to rid yourself of lingering anger, hostility or resentment.

You can ask for ways in which you can improve your morals, encourage morality and develop character. Be honest about what it is that you want to change in yourself before or after you've come to terms with it to help improve the overall quality of life. Then, ask yourself what is necessary to establish peace, happiness and wellbeing. Include personal improvements in your own as well as in the lives of those around you. Pray for those that have hurt you, those who have helped you and those that you love. Perhaps they are praying for you, too!

Pray every day and ask for ways in which you can be more loving, kind, honest, compassionate, to increase in prayer, but most of all, to understand what is truly necessary in life. Praying for wisdom and understanding in all circumstances and situations brings us closer to our true spiritual nature and the spiritual nature of others.

I think we have to realize that we can't rely on ourselves to control everything. We need to believe in a higher force that is supreme, all-loving and perfect.

As an educator and teacher in a country of religious tolerance and freedom I needed to learn early in my career how to make certain that my classes, courses, subject matter, and instruction were non-sectarian and without any personal religious bias or belief. This is a challenge for an individual but one that is readily met with the application of time and teaching discipline. However, it remains personally clear to me that we need to give up some of our earthly control and pray for spiritual importance and substance.

Often we are given spiritual tests in life to see how we can handle sometimes difficult situations. Life is also a test of our strengths, weaknesses and ultimate sense and practice of morality. When we begin to accept a higher spiritual authority, we begin to better understand and then accept ourselves as we really are and then in relation to each other. I have yet to find myself weakened instead of strengthened when embracing moral challenge in life. Moral victories are often the most exhilarating of all.

There is so much in life to learn. The continuum of life is about human struggle and our relationship to the divine. Understanding this fact brings us quickly to that higher spiritual plane and can fill us with the power to accomplish nearly anything we choose to master. Prayer can be the bridge between those ultimate forces of power and strength and our often own weaker and of course, more human existence and being.

Utilizing and extending that power makes us true artists of life. We can attain higher spiritual dimensions through prayer and by employing the greater virtues. With positive spiritual force on our side we can better create. And, create in a more magical, mystical, mysterious, and majestic way.

It takes time but we can gain insight and receive spiritual cleansing through prayer and the application of its benefits. So, don't get frustrated if your journey towards spirituality is gradual or has setbacks. Just be persistent in prayer.

Although I personally doubt that there is time in the spiritual dimension, there is in our own human existence. The answer from beyond can come to you quietly or like a bolt of lightning but still take time to re-deploy or implement. Remember, when it is time for you to become more insightful and more spiritually aware you will. However, this is only if you can remain open to the spiritual benefits and value of prayer.

# Chapter Twenty-four

## Self-appraisal and Appreciation

At one time or another we have all realized that we need to make friends and acquaintances happy. We tend to want to please other people. We may also have a tendency to boast or brag about our material possessions in an attempt to make others hold us in higher esteem. Sometimes we feel that we need to compete with a friend or relative to solidify our material status in comparison or in life.

Of course it's important to be good and to help others. It is also fulfilling and beneficial to be well-respected. That respect, however, should arise from genuine not just worldly success or accomplishments.

It is important to learn that you first need to be good to yourself and spend quality time doing things that you really enjoy, like exploring a new interest, hobby or fulfilling a passion. If you're not good to yourself and don't have a strong belief in who you are then how can you possibly be good to others? The answer is you can't.

Being good to yourself is recognizing how and why you are special, gifted or talented. An objective belief in oneself translates into the ability to have a powerful influence on the world and the lives of others through those gifts. You probably aren't aware of hidden qualities that you have that might make you special, and you never will until you explore. Whether it is doing something to improve your character or relationships, or learning how to properly help a friend or someone in need, the practical application of simple values is a good way to better understand yourself. Being good to yourself and others one day at a time will develop into being good to yourself and others in general and as a course of life.

Right appreciation of oneself may also come from reading good books, going back to school to study a favorite subject or taking trips to interesting places. Maybe you've decided to participate in a dance class, or see a new play, attend a symphony or opera, develop an interest in sports or art, or write a new business plan. It's all about new beginnings and keeping it simple. That is getting to know yourself better and then understanding how to nurture that very same self.

Whether you are a musician, writing music or a play, developing a new love relationship, or just becoming reacquainted with an old friend, doing something that will advance your overall positive personal outlook is another form of being good to oneself. You feel better about yourself by accepting yourself as who you are even with imperfections and flaws while at the same time not allowing shortcomings to get in the way with properly communicating with others. Only by first recognizing our own flaws can we begin to correct them and then, assisting with those of others.

By being good to yourself one step at a time you will eventually recognize and be in better tune with your true inner nature. By getting to know yourself better you will recognize the higher qualities in life to which you might like to aspire.

Give yourself a good self-appraisal by writing down all the things that you treasure and like about yourself. Then write the things that you don't like. What is it that you would want to add to the column of good qualities that you might already possess? What would you first like to remove from the column of things that you don't like about yourself? Now, how could you go about that step-by-step? Can you eventually eliminate the second column entirely? If not, why?

By being good to yourself you will get to know yourself better, discover ways of reshaping your life, properly modulate the good and bad traits that you have listed, and approach that spiritual plateau.

Do you know your strengths and weaknesses? Make another column for each. What is it in your life that you want to conquer? By being good to yourself, self-image will be restored, your character will advance, your perspectives in life will develop, and you will be better appreciated by others. Work on it. And, then work on the strengths and weaknesses, one at a time. It just takes personal concern and perseverance.

Find new interests or desires, attend group meetings with others who have similar likes or dislikes, seek secular or religious counseling, or even opt for psychotherapy. Develop a new image: positive, loving and caring. Suddenly everything begins to fall into place correctly and problems that linger are better understood and more manageable.

You will certainly gain more self-confidence and awareness along the way and eventually beam with beautiful lights and colors of self-fulfillment. You'll know that your spirit is alive and active within and that you are indeed reaching a higher plateau.

# Chapter Twenty-five

## Faith, Hope and Grace

The power to believe in something higher than oneself will give you a sense and feeling of peace. That aspiration to the divine is faith. Faith fills the voids of doubt and fear that you have about yourself, others and life in general and offers hope for a brighter tomorrow.

Faith or faiths are multi-faceted and universal. Faith itself is something that can't be seen with the physical eye but can be understood though a spiritual eye, hoped for and believed. The power of positive thoughts and positive energy brings positive results through faith.

Faith is belief in something that is not necessarily supported by direct evidence but substantiated by wisdom, understanding and truth. You can't actually put your finger on it but you know that it's there. That's faith.

In these same ways it is also like the two other great theological virtues: hope and charity. Together, these three theological virtues are attributed to belief in God.

Faith relates to being taken care of by a higher spiritual power, and through prayer and faith, one can attain grace. Grace is the special spiritual gift to achieve the unachievable, to persevere in the face of adversity and to conquer sin and transgression. This includes sin not only within oneself but also in others, and ultimately, in the world. It is the power to attain the otherwise unattainable and the ability to recognize and understand the better meaning of truth.

Hope can be defined as a Divine virtue by which we trust with confidence on Divine assistance and aspiration to achieve God's will for eternal life, truth and happiness. It is a theological virtue and comes with grace to accomplish and achieve. It is a strong positive force for good not only in our own life but also in the lives of others.

The combination of faith, hope, charity, and grace will help you understand the totality of your own existence and point you in a very special direction, adding self-appreciation and purpose to life. It is a great feeling to have purpose in life because purpose adds value and true value is a recognizable attribute. It raises existence in the world to the art of living life to the fullest, not only for our own enjoyment but again for the benefit of others.

What you couldn't understand before becomes easier if you can put your heart and mind behind the concepts of faith and grace. Grace will enhance the progress of your spiritual development. It can turn all negative thoughts and inclinations into positive thinking hopes and beliefs. These can and will happen for a higher purpose. That higher purpose adds more meaning to everyday existence and can improve the quality of your life in each and every significant way. You will understand your thoughts more clearly and ultimately be able to come to terms with self in all its good, bad and even indifferent ways.

If there are just two things in life that you should desire, aspire to and pray for, they are faith and grace. This is because through faith and grace, everything else is possible.

Do you feel sometimes that you would like to help someone? This could mean a friend, enemy, family member, or a stranger. Well, grace can provide you with the strength and eventually the means and the opportunity to accomplish good for your neighbor.

It's a positive attribute to contribute to the lives of others and thus to society at large. If there is a word that can describe the experience of helping someone that is ill or somehow in need, it would be compassion. Compassion is showing sympathy or kindness for someone else. Feeling something inside and bonding with that person goes beyond compassion and is called empathy. In either case, doing something good for someone else and expecting nothing in return is charity. And, charity is synonymous with love, coming from true belief and grace.

What you gain from this experience is satisfaction. That satisfaction is derived from doing something special which extends outside of oneself and can only remain fulfilling.

Whether it is doing volunteer work or raising money for a not-for-profit organization, when you recognize that you have done something out of compassion or rectitude you will want to continue to do more. This, too, elevates you spiritually, while contributing to the overall quality and well-guided power and art of living.

# Chapter Twenty-six

## Moral Principles and Values

Being cognizant and fully aware of our character defects can either lead to complacency, which is actually a continuing erosion of personal values in time, or action. By gaining increased knowledge about our strengths and weaknesses we can strive to do right and become a more developed person. As in our trip from teenage years to adulthood, the application of moral principles is as relevant then as it is now. The exercise of these principles is necessary to reach full development.

Are you ready to admit that you have character defects, flaws and are ready for a physical, mental and spiritual journey to come to truer terms with yourself? All the bad and mean things that you have either done to yourself or others have influenced who you really are today. They will continue to adversely affect you in life if you don't someday come to proper terms with them.

You should be able to come to a point of self-reflection and self-recognition where you can admit that you were wrong and should have handled certain situations differently. Can you admit that you have been at times inane, inactive, insensitive, or even insane and would like to right the circumstances? If you can, then you are ready to put all the bad parts of your character into an empty pitcher, pour it out and then all down the drain.

One should always grow in appreciation of what love and respect entail. You should be ready to study, develop and otherwise research or explore what perseverance, thanksgiving, patience, truth, honesty, and devotion are. How about further character development, as in true religiosity, right obedience, courtesy, loyalty, fortitude, heroism, and respect? Begin by living up to just some of these righteous words and concepts and then finding ways to apply them in your everyday life.

If you can gradually relate just some of these words and develop their concepts, you are on your way to learning the positive qualities that make us better individuals with a foundation of moral principles upon which to build.

We come out of the womb with a clear, open minded willingness to adapt and learn. Contemplate how these terms can balance both your internal and external states with natural balance and harmony as when life begins. Life like birth is filled with love, compassion, kindness, tenderness, straight forwardness, and instinctive eagerness to learn.

Only you can be willing to make a change. As we have learned the physical, so we must be willing to practice the spiritual. One can and will assist the other.

You have the ability and can eventually develop the disciplined and effortless state where you will be who and what you want to be. How you get there is only the fulfillment of the vision you employ. That vision is based upon all the points we have mentioned up until now, coupled with the practice of self-discipline and perseverance. All these points are keys, and each of these keys unlocks another part of our physical, emotional, mental, and spiritual self. Each is a small step toward attaining spiritual enlightenment which makes the continuation process all the easier. You have to take that first step and as you do, recognize the fact that you are really developing and practicing moral principles each successive step along the way.

Also along the way, don't forget to be grateful. Somehow, gratitude opens the doors to another form of moral development. Whenever I have felt truly grateful toward myself or others in life I have become further inspired. That inspiration provides resource and direction, leading to an even new path of growth and development.

Gratitude is a very moral expression of recognition. Often, we take things for granted and forget about those people who are good to us and what they have done. We need to give thanks for and to the people who have helped us during the good and bad times in our lives. This includes as well those who have had positive influences in any way.

Remember those who have given you moral encouragement and direction? This can include parents, friends, relatives, co-workers, teachers, or anyone from whom you might have learned. Giving someone thanks when it is due goes a long way. And, giving praise to a higher being or authority along the way from a kindred, inspired and satisfied heart only adds to one's joy.

Regrettably, many people today lack the inclination to inspiration or seek it from the wrong places. True inspiration is moral and especially important to emotional and spiritual wellbeing. It also helps with intellectual pursuits because it imparts a dimension in the realm of mental stimulation that can make us more creative.

Moral inspiration, power and values help develop physical prowess which is excellent for overall strength and endurance, especially when faced with danger. It can impart bravery and hope when confronted by opposition. These attributes are moral and fostered by inspiration.

Being open to right inspiration, from within and from without, from people and from life experiences, can strengthen your determination to grow. It will also allow you to remain steadfast in times of confusion and to sustain the moral principles and values that you have understood and developed along the way.

# Chapter Twenty-seven

## Inner Strength and Courage

The power that makes you want to succeed and that gives you that ultimate advantage is called strength. When you feel like you want to give up, a power far beyond just the ordinary takes over. Even if your physical body is tired, your spirit can kick in with inner strength and keep you going and well.

If life is a test and you've developed true inner strength and courage, you can conquer anything. You will have passed one of life's hardest examinations, that is the trial of perseverance. This means to keep going against all odds and obstacles, hurtles or pressure that may confront you. As the German philosopher Nietzsche once stated, "That which does not destroy you will make you stronger." The more inner strength you attain, the easier it will be to overcome unpleasant situations and difficulties.

Everyone knows and probably most people understand that love is the source of all positive energy. Love and kindness develop positive attitude and behavior. It helps you develop your inner abilities and strengths to keep thinking positive thoughts and developing morality with a truer sense of universal principle and purpose.

Courage on the other hand will help you to develop a non-quitting attitude and give you the ability to take risks that may change the course of your life for the best. Courage can supply the ability to improve the quality of life, while gaining and sustaining inner strength.

# Chapter Twenty-eight

## Relationships, Commitment and Friendship

There is much to be said about personal relationships. We need them especially to survive spiritually and emotionally. Social isolation is not for everyone. Having people to talk and relate to is what the power of life is very much about. It's about sharing life's gifts, insights, passions, and dreams.

Many medical experts feel that it is unhealthy to be alone too often because it deprives an individual of alternative emotional and mental stimulation. Committing to new friendships is important for new growth, particularly if the relationship is nurturing, meaningful and of lasting value.

Commitment to friendships and relationships, or anything that you set your mind to achieve at the personal level, will undoubtedly broaden and enrich your life. Like anything else, commitment takes work, patience and time. You need to put time and effort into building any relationship. You also need to dedicate yourself to anything that you believe in to follow it through.

The rewards of dedication can be everlasting. The benefits of good friendships will increase peace of mind, stimulate joy and encourage new attributes for development. Improved relationships also help the world become a much better and safer place in which to live and thrive.

# Chapter Twenty-nine

## A Sense of Humor

What would life be like without humor? I would think that it would be extremely dull. When there is always laughter and great fun, each day offers new moments and new experiences. And, you can find laughter in almost any person or non-tragic event.

Since each day is unique we can make the mundane and nearly any other situation come alive with laughter. People need laughter in their lives and should become less serious about the events that they come in contact with. Laughter keeps us young and vibrant as well as fresh with new insights. It is a good sense of humor that enlivens and encourages laughter.

Have a good laugh today. It should only help you develop a better sense of humor to appreciate and share tomorrow.

# Chapter Thirty

## Competition within Oneself

Many people have the need to compete with someone to show that they are better in a sport or for that matter, in any other aspect of life. They have a competitive nature and a need to keep up with the next person at all times. They are often competing for a financial edge or some other advantage over someone else. They develop a type 'A' personality and feel the need to always be right, always be perfect and always be in control. I'm sure that you know the person or mentality that I'm describing.

Once these individuals get what they want, they need more. They must always find a new challenge or someone else to compete with or against.

The competitive edge is good to a point but when it begins to consume you, beware that you have reached a spiritual impasse. The nature of competition is the ability to compete with your own true nature, yourself, rather than building up status and security with self-serving needs at the expense of others.

Competition can go much further in your life if you first challenge yourself with healthy goals and aspirations. As you grow physically, emotionally, mentally, and spiritually, the motives behind competition become very clear. The notions of self-improvement and universality become integral to your development and begin to sustain the lives of those around you. The more that you compete with yourself for higher knowledge and nobler purposes, the more gratified and enriched you will become. You will feel a genuine sense of empowerment and eventually an even-keeled ability on a much higher moral plane. You will also become better recognized in a beneficent way for your accomplishments.

If you're on a quest for self-exploration and self-improvement with motives sincere in nature, there isn't much that you can't strive for and accomplish. A little dedication each day to something that you believe in is the way in which you can compete with yourself. Eventually the good results will accumulate and you can adapt your goals and objectives in a clearer, more succinct and successive way. Living becomes an art and you quickly develop the knack of improving one aspect of your life after another. Suddenly, competition becomes linked to truth and understanding and is readily relatable to what you are doing in daily life, freeing and then lifting you out of routines and into real more spiritual realms of development.

Discipline will help you along this path. It will provide you with the opportunity to persevere and challenge you to acquire the higher attributes in life. This in turn lays the foundation and supports the underpinnings of good behaviors, supporting you on that higher plateau as you streamline your pursuit of the positively inevitable as well as once unattainable, with dreams that have longed to be fulfilled.

# Chapter Thirty-one

Physical fitness has always been an integral part of my life. From elementary school to present day fitness and wellbeing have encouraged me to be aware of the ongoing state of my health and have encouraged me to assist those who choose to get into better physical shape. I never miss a day of training and see it as a serious motivator for myself and others.

If some can gradually climb mountains you can gradually get into shape. Did you know that you already have the answers? They are within. It just takes time and application for them to emerge. If you can take one step, then two and three steps, it all becomes simple and truly progressive. If you try hard you will be able to make connections between the mind and its relationship to the workings of the body. It's not as intricate as it may seem and it all works in proper union together by nature, harmoniously.

If your mind isn't in a peaceful state you can't train your body to reach its utmost potential. The human body is an amazing creation and equally amazing is the way that it works. In one way or another, you must develop your mind and train your body with the utmost respect.

Our body is created as a pure temple in which the true spirit dwells. We need to keep it that way. To do so, we need to conquer the deficiencies or weaknesses that we can in our lives. One way is through the development of a stronger and more powerful body.

In many ways I feel that I am in at least as good physical shape today as I was twenty years ago. I attribute this to strong discipline, dedication, commitment, and follow-through in what I believe. Once you believe in something you can make it happen. Practicing the physical disciplines and employing the greater virtues makes so very much of this possible. If you have setbacks, you can try harder or appeal to a higher or divine nature to get back onto the right course.

I believe that physical fitness is a true extension of oneself because not only can it reflect your own being, but it can also positively affect the lives of those people that surround you. Many great masters with exceptional wisdom teach and explain that fitness goes beyond the physical dimensions. So, what you can't see with your physical eye still transcends the capacity of your physical work.

I can move very well with my students. Each time I teach a class I'll do everything with them so that I can still feel proud, sharing the joy with them that they have succeeded.

Physical fitness can improve your mood, relax your body and mind, keep you centered, put a smile on your face, help you perform better in your studies, improve overall achievement levels, give you better focus, and provide a sense of determination, accomplishment, fulfillment, joy, and peace within yourself. In the end proper physical fitness can not only help make you a better person but also help sustain your existence on a spiritual plateau. There is no end to the accomplishments that you can make with good physical fitness.

What could be better than lowering your cholesterol, your blood pressure if it is too high or becoming more limber and flexible? There is nothing that can't be attained in your life if you put the commitment, discipline, drive, and hard work into what you are correctly pursuing.

Physical fitness can help you achieve development in each and every muscle in your body. You will be more agile and confident about the ways in which you can move your body and be able to perform better when you are fit. This can only help you feel good about yourself and better able to become physically, emotionally, mentally, and spiritually developed.

All baseball, football, basketball, volleyball, tennis, soccer, or whatever sport you play, has some physical fitness principles built into the program. Some teams need more fitness than others. Most martial arts programs like taekwondo, karate, aikido, kung fu, kick boxing, boxing, or wrestling have fitness programs associated with them. Yoga, cardio fitness, Pilates, and dance all have fitness and warm-up exercises.

If you are not a member of a team, club or gym and want to get into some form of improved physical shape you can practice any of the disciplines that I have outlined as a beginning, just as a child can understand and develop. If you are a member of a team, club, gym, or even martial art school, I hope that you will find some value in new ways of looking at fitness.

How many people that you know have over-trained, did not stretch out properly, hurt their back, had knee surgery, have had tendonitis in their arm, or broke a leg, ankle or arm while skiing or in a competitive game? I can say I know quite a few of these people. Thank goodness that through all the years I've been working out or training another that I have never sustained a major physical injury.

Part of this has to do with knowing your body and what your limitations are. People have asked me over the years,

"How much should I work out?" The answer is always personal and also depends on the age and the condition of the person including their body as well as overall physical emotional and mental states of being. Remember, ask your general practitioner this very same question.

There are various ways in which you can improve the overall quality of your life through physical fitness. Whether you are a child, teenager, young adult, approaching middle age, or even an elderly person, you should learn a discipline like a martial art, a dance, train in a fitness class, join a gym, play a sport, enjoy a daily walk or jog, or just do whatever you and a professional decide is a right beginning to improved physical wellbeing.

We know that some people who have participated in certain active team sports can no longer play them as well as when they were younger, or even at all. By all means couch that activity and be involved physically with your kids, friends or others. There are always certain activities that you can engage in and practice to maintain or improve your physical wellbeing. Sports like golf, tennis, croquet, volleyball, racquetball, and badminton offer less strenuous exercise and are often played well into adulthood.

Young or old, some of the internal or softer martial art styles such as kung fu, tai chi chuan, chi gung, and paqua breathing method, are graceful and offer great fitness value. Some soft karate styles such as yoga styles with stretching, breathing exercises and meditation offer relaxation, focus and agility. Aikido, another great martial art, also offers exceptional exercise, body movement skills and a great sense of mental discipline.

One difference between a martial art and a sport is that sports are mainly physical and mental while martial arts are physical, mental and offer spiritual connection. That spirituality no matter how it manifests itself puts us back in touch with our better nature and should provide further insight into life in general. Whether from the East or the West anyone can merge spiritual forces and incline them to complementary physical, mental or spiritual realms of accomplishment by also practicing the higher virtues.

# Chapter Thirty-two

There are many martial art disciplines. What are they and what do they offer? I will try to describe a significant handful:

**Aikido** is an unarmed method of self defense where you use your body weight against the other person's balance without using undo strength while gaining control. One can add strength through various aikido exercises such as bending and twisting joints and limbs.

Training can develop a positive attitude and in time you will develop 'ki' which is known as internal power: the vital force that we all achieve and strive for. It's a power that comes from inside the body.

You can move your body in many directions when you study this graceful art and you can move your opponent in many directions as well. Coordination, agility and hand-eye coordination will improve through practice. In many respects the movements are similar to dance because they are fluid and continuous. There is also a continual flow of energy and motion.

**Karate** is a discipline that has Japanese, Okinawan and American styles and can provide an overall workout for the mind and body. You will learn how to stand properly, move your body in different patterns similar to dance and experience a great cardiovascular workout from the constant movement of kicking, punching, striking, and blocking.

Karate translated means "empty hand." In a deeper way, its definition is emptying your mind from clutter and distraction and removing all preconceived thoughts so that you are able to learn and accomplish. Once your mind is empty of thought you can begin to learn. Fifty percent are your hands which are very specially directed and fifty percent are your feet. You learn when to attack in the offensive position and learn how to defend in the defensive position as well.

**Taekwondo** is a Korean martial art that emphasizes eighty percent kicking and twenty percent hand techniques. It's actually an approved Olympic sport. Much emphasis is placed on jumping and kicking drills.

Taekwondo students practice a great deal of stretching so that they are extremely flexible when they kick. It's a great exercise and a superb workout. The art works on generating momentum with spinning so that the kicks are fluid, incorporating great body dynamics.

**Judo** is a Japanese martial art and worldwide sport. It involves throwing techniques, arm and leg locks, holdings on the mat, choke holds, and of course, sparring. The art boasts many grappling techniques such as wrestling and self-defense counters for self-protection. Judo is a great workout emphasizing stress endurance, power, strength, and alertness. The art builds stamina and improves balance.

**Jujitsu** is also an art with a Japanese background. It is a combination of judo and karate. It involves strikes, takedowns, grappling, and submission to the mat. Defending yourself against bare hand and against weapons is prevalent in this art. Kicking and punching, hold downs and joint locks are also popular. This art is excellent to practice because it compliments many karate techniques. It takes perseverance and a great deal of motivation to learn.

**Hapkido** is a Korean self-defense art that involves striking, kicking and wrist seizures. It has elements of judo in movement of power and is like Aikido in terms of leverage and balance. Hapkido, like Aikido, uses circular techniques to break down an opponent's balance.

**Kung fu** is a Chinese martial art that represents movements derived from different animals such as the monkey, dragon, tiger, lion, crane, praying mantis, and swan. There are many styles of kung fu like in karate. Some are hard external styles that emphasize external power. Other styles are more internal and concentrate on developing power from within. Internal energy is concentrated on softer, slower and calmer motions while the external styles are more strenuous, forceful and become faster transitions.

Kung fu is complex, intricate yet simplistic in its movements and is an art similar to painting that can have diverse meanings. Kung fu is a dance, a self defense, an exercise, a philosophy, and like other martial arts, is great for developing overall good health and stamina.

**Tai chi chuan** is a graceful martial art that is practiced in slow motion to develop harmony and stillness, while at the same time giving the practitioner a great internal and external workout. The internal workout develops the mind and emotional state. The inner movements are beautiful and represent tranquility and a harmonious union between the mind, body and spirit. The external contains the exercise and stretching in movement that benefits dexterity and overall strength.

**Chi kung** is often practiced simultaneously with tai chi chuan. Others practice this Chinese breathing exercise to become centered. It emphasizes slow breathing exercises, meditation and floor as well as standing exercises.

**Ninjitsu** is an old feudal Japanese secret fighting system which incorporates weapons, evasion, invisibility, mystical experiences, and developing energy from the world and earth made up of water, fire, metal, and wind. It utilizes Bushido, espionage, commando warfare, camouflage, and pressure point attacks to vital parts of the body. The art emphasizes numerous martial arts disciplines.

**Kendo** is the art of using a bamboo shinai or sword to practice strikes and blocks. It is both a sport and discipline. Its objectives are to land two scoring blows to vital target areas. It's a great workout because you remain in constant motion. You have to be in shape to practice this art. Or, eventually you will get in shape because of the great dedication that development in the art requires.

**Iaido** is the Japanese art of sword. It involves drawing the blade, proper stances, cuts, and strikes. The art develops great posture and flexibility and has a singularly disciplinary element because when you draw the blade it is just you and the blade.

Drawing the blade is a straightforward motion; a clean and direct way of being sincere to yourself and others. The thought is to cut, slice, strike, and return to the beginning. There are no false pretenses, illusions or any way of altering this particular exercise.

Iaido, the sword, keeps you on track to know when to attack and when to withdraw. Its motives are authentic and genuine. The way you practice this art is the way you can begin living your life: free of confusion, uncertainty and awkwardness.

**Wrestling** deals with discipline, willpower and the ability to lose weight. It also involves mental toughness to sustain yourself during each bout in a similar way that karate training teaches you to have a strong spirit and strong will. If you're a wrestler you know that you have to take down your opponent, put him on his back and keep him there for a few seconds to win the match.

This same holds true in life. To succeed you have to believe in what you're doing, follow through to its conclusion and be able to go along with the change of others as you change yourself.

**Western boxing** deals with punching, conditioning, jumping rope, and bag training. These techniques work with combinations of punches in relation to various methods for shifting the body.

Similarly, each aspect of an art has positive points. You can learn anything from any art or discipline as long as you put the effort, patience and dedication to study.

**Kickboxing** is a rough fighting method, bear knuckle, and bear fist. Kicks to the legs and knees are quite possible. Being elbowed is not uncommon and being kicked or punched in the face is possible in any of the more exuding physical encounters.

You probably wonder why people might be attracted to this exercise or sport. Some can get past the brutality because they were fighters on the street to begin with. They find this art as a challenge, like a competition to test their skills. You have to be in good shape, quick, agile, strong, and have a strong spirit to survive this type of competition.

**Cardio-kick boxing** is kick boxing to music or exercises with kicks and punches. It's a great workout because you are getting your heart rate up. It is a fun workout that concentrates on the improvement of your physical appearance and your overall conditioning.

Not only do you go through the rigorous kicking and punching drills, but you get a chance to practice your moves on another person with hand and feet pads. This reduces the chances of injuries.

There is very much power that goes into practicing and executing these sets of techniques. The willingness to be able to carry out specific practices demonstrates courage and provides benefit to a total workout program.

This workout also stimulates both your body and mind. In fact most of these disciplines improve body, mind and spirit connection. Efforts extended during workout programs will provide the results of positive energy, improved physical strength and improved physical, mental and emotional wellbeing.

**Yoga** is very popular today and will continue to be so because of its wide range of disciplines. There are many schools of thought on the way yoga should be taught. Some practice it with stretching, salutations, prayer, and meditation. Others practice it with a more cardiovascular workout approach.

There are also many singular postures in yoga. And, there are many ways that you can move your body from different standing, kneeling and sitting positions.

Yoga takes on many forms and is a great way to develop good posture, dexterity, balance, and conditioning. It's also a total centering discipline that is highly motivated by spirituality combined with mind and body coordination. It's a lifestyle for some and a spiritual journey for others.

Yoga makes you feel better about yourself and therefore can improve interpersonal relationships. In addition to being a great way to stay in shape, yoga stresses moderation and fortitude which can improve attitude and stamina. It develops ethical principles such as character, love, humility, and heroism.

Yoga, as well as the other martial arts, is also about improving the quality of your life in all areas from health and friendships to significant relationships. The martial arts in general foster learning and higher knowledge as well as pursuit of new endeavors. Yoga teaches you about being open and honest with your feelings and emotions. It provides you with a straightforward truthful approach to living life.

**Competitive sports** or club activities are a great way to workout and develop team-spirited relationships. Whatever it may be: a soccer game, swimming, marathon, or volleyball game, you should give it your all. It could be football, baseball, basketball, golf, or tennis, anything, including bowling.

The important point to understand here is that you are exercising and accomplishing a good workout as well as learning skill and technique. You are also relating to other people. However, make certain that you warm up for a while before playing any competitive sport.

**Dance** is a powerful art and exercise. There are many styles of dance from many diverse cultural backgrounds. Here again you are learning about yourself, your strengths and weaknesses.

You can soon realize how an imperfect and awkward move can become more graceful, taking you along the way toward perfection. Dance can work many major as well as minor muscle groups making you stronger, more agile, flexible, and of course provide you with added stamina and energy.

Some of the movements are interconnected with those of martial art styles. Each martial art style like kung fu, karate or aikido is similar in one aspect or another to dance because of the fluidity, patterns and flow.

Dance can also be extremely creative and has great benefits for overall body conditioning as well as relaxation. Any good dance class can provide stimulation and rewards far greater than you can imagine. Some of the rewards can be the centering of the mind and body as well as the ability to develop a positive influence for yourself through better movement and balance, even in approach toward life.

**Aerobics and similar disciplines** such as aquatics, cardio-fitness, cardio-kick boxing, taebo, karobics (a mixture of karate and dance), aero-boxing (a mixture of boxing and aerobics), and Pilates (a great workout involving stretching and exercises that work most of your muscle groups, many simultaneously) are each exercises and sets of exercises that can be extraordinarily beneficial.

**Gyms** with treadmills, elliptical machines, rowing machines, cycle machines, stair masters, or any machine that you feel you are getting an effective total workout from can also become a good discipline for physical wellbeing. As long as you don't overdo the beginnings you can gradually increase and benefit from each and every workout module.

Make sure to rotate from machine-to-machine. Certain days you can work different muscle groups and make certain to alternate each week. One day you can work the chest area, two days later work the legs and then next the back and then shoulders so that you eventually get a full workout. This method of training will provide improved strength, greater endurance and result in overall good muscle tone.

**Weight training** can also tone your body. It is very effective in developing strength, balance and power. If you are not training in a competition but want to feel as though you are making progress, then you need to lift every other day. Work with weights that you feel comfortable with, don't strain yourself, don't show off, and when you feel the burn, stop.

In all these disciplines, there are both practical and applicable aspects that when combined with other disciplines develop physical, emotional, mental, and eventually spiritual attributes. It is really a step-through process to reach a higher level of appreciation in all aspects of human development and understanding. Remember, one state of being cannot remain isolated from another.

In the end mind, body and spirit connection becomes both integral and seamless. This takes times, hard work, perseverance, and the application of higher qualities and higher values and virtues to truly accomplish. However, the wholeness that emerges as a result is so unique, measurable, fulfilling, and consistent with human as well as divine expectations that quality of life improvements will become not just an occurrence or endurance but a way of living life as an art.

In many ways it can all seem a bit overpowering or difficult to initially comprehend. Well, just begin the journey and you will soon be able to understand as well as appreciate that each singular gain is not only one special one but a significant part of cumulative experience. One gain after another supports goals of accomplishment that are ultimately applicable to any way of life.

*Far right, Teddy Smith*

*Soshu Shigeru Oyama and Teddy Smith*

*Master Peter Urban*

*Master Richard Kim*

*Master Aaron Banks and Teddy Smith*

*Teddy Smith, Seido Karate Dojo, New York*

# Chapter Thirty-three

Life is a continuum that should employ character development, ethics, morality, inspiration, improved interpersonal relationships, communication, and higher qualities and values. Since your behavior affects how you will progress in life, let's have a quick reality check or an understanding of what reality means.

If reality is a state of mind then what mindset do you have? Reality is life without a state of confusion, seeing clearly without illusions. It's what is real, within and without. So, if you're living your life with too many illusions or unfulfilled dreams then your chance of physical, emotional, mental, and ultimately spiritual growth will remain nominal. In other words, these gains won't find foundation in reality.

As explained from the beginning, if you can wipe your life clean of distraction and confusion, it would be easier to live free of future clutter and disorder, without disoriented or distorted thoughts. Many people that have you have met in your life may seem so busy that they don't have the time to do anything but what they are self-involved with, never allowing themselves the opportunity to work instead on self-development and improvement. Take the time yourself and even if it's just a half-an-hour a day, use it to improve the dimensions of your own life. Just think what a great life you can have if you both integrate as well as enliven the greater potential within that each of us possess and should share.

To be a person of higher quality you first have to distinguish between good and bad character and then apply better values to all life experiences. Good character is the result of the good values and qualities that we have and practice in our lives. Do you have good traits that are sincerely motivated and utilized with integrity?

There are many righteous words that have significant value in life. Words and the concepts behind them can be lived up to with right action. That can be called righteousness. It's a gradual process, a struggle and a redefining process that not only determines what is important in your life but again, also in the lives of others.

Righteous words such as: love, perseverance, thanksgiving, patience, integrity, truth, honesty, and true accomplishment are necessary to advance the development of your spirit.

Satisfaction, happiness, religion, obedience, courtesy, loyalty, fortitude, politeness, gratitude, respect, heroism, and rectitude are necessary for the improvement of the quality of your life as well as the enrichment of spirit and soul.

Wisdom, understanding, intuition, and insight are also important words as well as concepts that humankind singularly or together should aspire. You can and should weave these terms into the fabric of everyday life.

The following are among the higher values represented by words that inspire the better qualities of life on the physical, mental, emotional, and spiritual plateaus:

**Love.** Love is integral to life. As it is the bridge between inner strength and courage, casting out fear and replacing it with faith and grace, so it affects you in just about every other way you can imagine. First, it is a divine gift. Second, it is the most powerful of human emotions. Thirdly, it is greater to give than to receive.

You may sometimes wonder how and why this particular emotion can affect your actions and enhance you spiritually. Love completes the totality of life.

You probably have met people who have said that they love you and then in a few months disappear. This is because they have used the term incorrectly. The true indication of a person's love is measured by their concerted actions.

Being there for a person through good and bad times is a form of right action. Love can be true friendship, platonic, romantic, intimate, and spiritual once you get past simply physical attraction. Love is also righteous, and offers good intentions, good actions, good motivation and is the inspiration behind good works. Importantly, it is given and humanly as well as divinely received.

Physical attraction alone is not real love, but you need an attraction to first spark romantic love. The attitudes, attributes and roots of attraction are obscure. Can you really figure out why you are physically attracted to someone? It's something beyond chemistry - - something beyond that which our finite minds fully comprehend. So much more is love.

You read about love in great literature. I not only believe that we can enliven this kind of love but also believe that it is a necessary attribute to complete life, or an area of your life to conquer. Without love you cannot be fulfilled, experience joy or understand what it means to exist on a higher spiritual plateau. This is so because love embodies higher attributes that are needed to sustain spiritual growth.

An objective love of one's self and an unselfish love of family, friends and neighbors are all necessary to employ the greater virtues and truly appreciate as well as succeed in life.

**Perseverance.** Perseverance is the will to continue whatever you chose without hesitation. Perseverance helps develop a strong spirit. If there's anything in life that you feel you can't accomplish, with perseverance you can. Perseverance turns weakness into strength. Persistence and follow-through are pre-requisites for accomplishment. They will make you stronger and will develop greater internal and external strength.

If you believe you're right, don't give in and don't give up. Follow your passions and dreams and make them reality through perseverance. Only you can make it happen. Keep trying and never give up, no matter what anyone else says, does or might incorrectly think.

**Thanksgiving.** I have always appreciated the word thanksgiving. In America, it is synonymous with the gift of our forefathers for their safe arrival in the New World. This gratitude and expression of hope holds powerful significance today, especially for the people who have influenced and inspired you. It's a way of expressing gratitude for the good others have offered.

Thanksgiving is about the people and events that have helped you and your way of recognizing them in return. Remember, even mean people as well as disturbing events have had something to teach you. They have made you stronger and hopefully, wiser.

One should always be ready to offer thanksgiving in prayer, praise and other actions. Through the practice of this particular virtue, we can continue the tradition of giving instead of receiving throughout our lives and encourage spiritual growth in ourselves and others.

**Patience.** They say that patience is a virtue and it is because with patience your spirit becomes calm, defined and better informed. Today, many people forsake patience and replace it with what they can have just for today or for now. Well, life doesn't always work that way.

The more patient you are, the better your life can become. Not all things come to us in life, and certainly not always when we desire or even expect them. Instant gratification is a flagrant social lie. For example, nothing in life can be really learned and properly absorbed that quickly. Then how can it be achieved? You need time to sit and contemplate important matters to arrive at significant conclusions. Therein resides well-earned gratification. And, it takes patience.

Take your time and be positive. If you don't get results instantly simply persist. Life is a gradual process that is constantly evolving. Knowledge is a lifelong process in the development, patience and accomplished within definitive virtue to beneficially achieve all.

**Integrity.** If you want to be in a wholesome relationship, you hope that the person will be faithful, honest and have integrity, which also means forthright and truthful. Without trust and integrity our relationships fall apart and we can no longer function in a framework of trust. Developing integrity reshapes and redefines character for the better. Integrity is a higher virtue and quality in life practiced by the goodly and most often those that are both righteous and remain very properly self-appraised.

**Truth.** Truth is one of the most important concepts in all of life. It is divine and universal. It affects each and every one of our decisions and judgments in life. Without truth, there is no correct knowledge, wisdom or justice.

You can choose the righteous path in life to tell and accept the truth, or the evil path to lie or believe in a lie. Truth leads us to the spiritual plateau, teaches us what is really important in life and can improve the quality of our daily lives in each, any and every way.

It's sometimes difficult to relate the truth but in the end it is much more difficult to lie. When you lie, your story changes several times and is not spiritually substantiated. In contrast, truth coincides with your true and spiritual nature, including sincerity and forthrightness. Lies are among the most unforgivable of transgressions, whereas truth always aspires to the magnificence of the divine.

Understanding and accepting truth can only change your life in a positive way. Conversely, believing or acting upon a lie will only lead to destruction. Truth provides balance and focus to all situations just as it also brings you closer to a natural state of internal and external peace. Truth will better align you with universality because the universe was created in beauty, truth and grace. Being in tune with the universe and one's self in truth is practicing the highest of virtues, those which emanate from the divine as they are inspired by beneficence and munificence.

**Honesty.** It is obviously better to be honest and upright rather than dishonest. And yes, honesty is a form of truth.

If you're not honest you are not accomplishing personal spiritual justice, which means that your physical, emotional and mental wellbeing are not more perfectly aligned. You can't understand yourself or build quality relationships unless you are honest.

You need to develop ethical behavior to be and stay in business. Without honesty to yourself and others you will cease to thrive. Others recognize truth and as a derivative, honesty. It's always better to be honest and straightforward as you develop a strong and powerful bond of good actions and right attitudes toward yourself and others in all aspects of life.

**Devotion.** Isn't it a great feeling to believe in something strongly and act it out in a positive way? When you are dedicated to a cause or anything that influences your life positively and have a strong allegiance to it, you do much better at it because you truly believe in what you are doing. It becomes easier to persevere, accomplish and eventually, succeed. All of this takes devotion.

**Obedience.** Life can be much more orderly when you are able to obey correct orders. Or, develop a structure in your family or organization where obedience to a righteous person, such as a parent or civil authority, becomes a matter of form. This isn't always easy and of course in practice, you need to remain correctly circumspect.

Being obedient to a group or within a corporation or organization is a sign of respect to the others who belong. Living life in accordance with local and national governmental laws to the best of your ability is also obedience, usually benefiting communal life which is of course, society. Obedience is connected with self-discipline because it improves the overall quality of the self through hard work, determination and ultimately, rectitude in form.

**Self-determination.** The virtue of self-determination deals with being strong, firm in resolve and true to a belief, goal or objective. It means being able to achieve what you set out to do. It is a necessary attribute for success in life as well as the proper practice of other greater virtues within the spectrum of learning the higher qualities that elevate us to the spiritual plateau.

**Contentment.** Sometimes people feel that they are never happy with what they are doing or have and always have needed to seek elsewhere or have more. Being content frees the mind of this unnecessary untruth and ensuing anguish and pain. 'Having' does not mean contentment and always looking elsewhere is not seeking in the right frame of reference. Being satisfied is being content and will lead to fulfillment, joy, satisfaction, gratification, and completeness. This is contentment.

**Respect.** Employing the virtue of respect means demonstrating well-deserved kindness toward another. When you are respectful, you are sincere, show gratitude, honor, concern, and value in dealing with others. When you give praise to others you extend a sense of self-worth beneficial to all humankind. It is also a sign of good conduct and deportment.

**Righteousness.** Righteousness is a combination of virtues such as goodness and truth. It is the perfecting of spirit as demonstrated in proper form and proper action. It is also the result of faith, grace and goodness. Without goodness there can never be righteousness.

**Rectitude.** This means right action and doing the right thing at the right time. It also is a virtuous response to certain situations. It benefits oneself because it is self-correcting in nature and others because it is developmental as both a gift and virtue.

**Compassion.** When you feel the pain of another, hold a specific empathy, learn to understand someone else's feelings, especially sorrow or anguish, and have a genuine place for that other person in your heart, you have compassion. This may kindle a spark or an awakening from your own experiences by learning through the suffering or sorrows of another. If you feel bad for someone's misfortune or illness and it affects you in a positive way, then you have learned from practicing the greater virtue of compassion.

**Happiness.** You read about happiness in literature, hear about it in music and are constantly offered it through media. What determines happiness is anyone's guess, but it emanates first from a state of personal equilibrium, calm and tranquility of nature.

Happiness comes from within. It's really not dependent on external information or stimuli as a matter of form. How what reaches us in terms of intellect, emotion or reasoning is processed and how the energy is received within will give us a better idea of whether or not we become happy. Happiness is almost always shared. And, another gift offered and received.

When we aren't happy we should initiate change and try to turn the mundane and life's insanity into something more pleasurable and rightfully prosperous. If we are fortunate enough to be healthy, can appreciate the beneficial lessons that life has to offer and are open and honest to our true nature and that of others, then there is already reason to be happy. Reflecting on what is truly important should also earn an inner smile that becomes happiness shortly or at least, with time.

**Joy.** Having a true sense of exuberance, even during difficult times, is to experience joy. It is the rising above pain and suffering to a place where happiness dwells with contentment and hope. Any experience can be turned into a positive in one way or another. With joy one can illuminate, dispelling potential unhappiness in ourselves and others. Joy is happiness and love, peace and contentment, and many other virtues, all with a special energy divinely dispersed as joy.

**Tolerance.** Tolerance is a word and concept that may be uncomfortable for many because it means being open to all of life's good and bad possibilities. It also requires discipline. Can you get beyond prejudice, ethnicity, race, color, and be accepting of people's problems and shortcomings? If you can you are able to learn more about your own shortcomings and become tolerant. Tolerance, like charity, should begin at home. In other words, within one's self.

By keeping an open perspective toward humanity you can see the goodness that transcends human weakness, differences and prejudice of any kind. Are you able to rise above intimidation, self-serving interests and be more tolerant and understanding of people's faults and weaknesses, including your own? If you can, or even make an inch of progress in this area, you are on the road to where practicing the virtue of tolerance becomes, like living on the spiritual plateau, a way of life.

**Politeness.** Politeness is being kind, short, sweet, accepting, loving, to the point, and all in a giving fashion.

**Courtesy.** Closely linked to politeness and respect, and often lacking in contemporary society, is the important attribute of courtesy which improves personal human relations, especially in more social context.

It also takes forgiveness and rectitude to be courteous, which implies continuing effort in its deployment. However, courteousness empowers both you and the recipient and makes you both feel special in other very virtuous ways.

It feels much better to be nice than mean, and then kinder to others. Try to explain this to someone who is mean or infrequently kind. He or she won't understand or properly respond to you at first because they will never afford you the courtesy. But, courteously, give them time.

**Heroism.** Heroism can be defined as courage, bravery, valiance, and doing something noble. Taking informed chances are necessary to improve the quality of relationships, careers, reputation, position in society, and being able to change in general. So too can taking a well-calculated even bigger chance prove to be heroic! If it fails then just pick yourself up and either try again or be a little less daring next time, or in another way.

Heroism is very much connected to help, and help is a necessary laudable virtue.

**Humility.** I appreciate the greater virtue of humility because it invokes so many meanings, connotations and implications. Another word that I particularly like with respect to humility is modesty.

I believe that you are respected more if you are a better listener than a bragger. Do you like it when people talk about themselves and really don't listen or care what you think or feel? It's good to be humble and respect another person's opinions and thoughts even though you may hold different ones.

Humility will make you more understanding, compassionate, bring you closer to truth, and in the end, help you develop a greater and much more evolved spiritual person.

**Gratitude.** It's always nice to get a thank you for all the good you have done to help someone. Or, at work, praise for your accomplishments. If it's truly better to give than receive than gratitude is the place to start.

**Forgiveness.** Holding onto grudges and hostility can make you mentally and physically ill. Spiritually, it means death. So, don't live without forgiveness. Have faith, belief and love in your body, spirit, soul, and mind. It will get you through all those rough and turbulent days. Make life a more bearable exercise not only for yourself, but also for others by learning and practicing to forgive.

**Loyalty.** It's great to be loyal, upright and straightforward, especially in a relationship, organization, a school, or even just a thought. Loyalty should accompany each and every relationship in life and will help accomplish life's journey with right acumen and ultimate success. It also very well benefits others.

**Passion.** True passion is exceptionally fulfilling and a powerful emotion. It is something far-reaching and represents spirit, body and mind connection, evoking an intense emotional experience. That experience can be, but is not necessarily, very related to nature. However, it is an emotion that can also be associated with work, family, friends, and a driving force in any proper path in life. Passion is good when it is well-controlled, properly directed and of course, well-tempered.

**Satisfaction.** It is important to feel good about what you do in life. Almost everything good is attainable. If you find that what you are doing isn't stimulating, gratifying or fulfilling then you need to look into other options that can enhance your personal and professional development. You'll know when you have made the right decision and found the right path when the feeling that results is satisfaction. Satisfaction leads to fulfillment, fulfillment to joy, and joy can enkindle spiritual enlightenment.

**Fortitude.** When you develop strength which comes from your body, mind and spirit it will translate into fortitude. As bad as things may seem, keep a positive outlook and find solace in what you do. Fortitude can help make this possible at all times.

Fortitude protects us from both internal and external transgression, extraordinary challenges and moral conflict of any and all sorts. It sustains us on our beneficial physical, emotional and mental paths, assists in our employing the greater virtues and helps us to maintain our existence on the spiritual plateau.

**Religion.** Whether or not you attend an organized religious service and in whatever good faith or denomination you choose to belong, religion is important to develop spirit, maintain good fellowship and strengthen ethical values. Importantly, it can help one maintain a proper self-perspective as well as correct improper attitude towards others. And, it is most frequently fundamental to the proper understanding of both the spiritual and especially, the divine.

**Generosity.** Did you ever feel better about yourself, or has someone ever explained how kind you are because you are a giving person? It is important to give of oneself - - first in spirit, second in truth and third in any other good way possible.

Life is a delicate balance and not just in one's own existence. Whenever that balance becomes offset it can cause unnecessary trouble. Extending goodness to someone in need can help re-establish life's ever-sustaining proper balance. All of this comes from a generous spirit and helps better define generosity.

**Kindness.** If you have the choice to be kind or mean which would you choose and why? Most people would choose to be kind. If, however, you have a poor self-image or need to protect your status quo or job in relation to others at the expense of using someone else, you are choosing to be mean.

There are many ways to be mean and it's most often a quick but simple choice to be kind instead. You will always be respected for choosing to be kind.

They say, "What goes around comes around." Kindness should become a matter of form like politeness and courtesy. If you want to help someone else, start by being kind. Acts of kindness also help to make the world a better place to live. And, can only benefit you in one way or another in time

**Motivation.** It is crucial to follow through on everything that you set out to do. You need to have interests and people around you that are fun, stimulating and educational.

Try to do the best job possible at home, in your work and set out to properly develop your friendships and relationships. The more affirmative your sense of purpose and design is, the better motivated you'll become. Motivation leads to self-determination, perseverance and fortitude and with these virtues, ensures that not only a circumstance or necessary situation gets addressed, but also accomplished properly.

**Wisdom.** Wisdom is among the greatest of all virtues. It is a very powerful word that cannot live apart from spirituality. Without an understanding of greater virtues and a right sense of spirituality there can be no wisdom.

It is also of great religious, moral and intellectual appreciation and goes beyond human understanding. It is the power of truth, understanding and grace that you can find on the spiritual plateau, but only as a divine gift. **Enlightenment.** Enlightenment is the awareness of spiritual truth and wisdom in ourselves and others. Have you ever become enlightened? Did someone transmit knowledge to you that you can remember and were able to adeptly and correctly apply for the rest of your life? There should always have been some or even many who have tapped or sparked an interest that has improved the quality of your life with enlightenment.

Enlightenment can seem to come from nowhere, but it doesn't just happen. It arrives as a special combination of the higher virtues, including truth, understanding and a very special kind of knowledge.

The truth that enlightenment imparts is real. The state of enlightenment brings life to a more harmonious balance and invites you to follow the righteous path to attain even further grace and enlightenment.

**Temperance.** This is a virtue that deals with the ability to moderate oneself, someone else or a situation using self-control. Living life in the middle, never giving in to extremes or not abusing substances like alcohol or drugs is exhibiting the quality of temperance. With temperance reality becomes a way of life, not a concept distorted by emotion or irreparability.

**Prudence.** You need to be careful how you pick your friends or the type of people you are involved with. Do these people offer you growth, positive reinforcement and good energy? The word prudence means to be careful. It also means knowing how to be able to read a person's true character and innate qualities. It forbids excess, commands respect and leads to moderation in human situations as well as interaction.

**Justice.** It is great to be treated fairly and of course with respect. How often are you treated with respect and equality? Treat people fairly because injustices can return in unpleasant and surprising ways. Give credit where it is due and be fair and upright when dealing with others.

The world was created in beauty and truth and justice is part of the natural universal state as well as equation. Consequently, injustice is something that is fought on the most instinctual level as well as the highest sociological as well as spiritual planes and plateaus.

On the spiritual level, justice is a predominate force. In life, and especially in afterlife, it is impossible to escape true justice.

**Insight.** Did you ever think that you could understand what someone is thinking or feeling? You may find that you have a special way of reading or perceiving the inner state of that person or a particular situation at-hand.

Good insight is knowledge that can't always be read or understood or even defined through theory. It is internalized as well as externalized and the knowledge that comes from its understanding is intuitive, instinctive and real.

**Intuition.** Being able to quickly understand a moment, situation, reality, or even part of a reality instinctively is intuition. Intuition understands the truth without necessarily using fact or even relying on the rational mind. You can often analyze a seemingly ambiguous situation or event using proper reasoning power with intuition. Understanding can come to life instinctively when you tap or try to apply good intuition.

**Accomplishment.** It is gratifying and enriching to complete something from beginning to end. You feel like you have made something worthwhile happen. You are happy and positive about it all. Success and feeling joy from that success brings with it positive energy and a sense of accomplishment. Accomplishment is a fulfillment and completion of something right. Accomplishment is also a feeling that exceeds most others, especially in a righteous way. And, as a proper end, it usually heralds a vital new beginning.

# Chapter Thirty-four

The mind can and will affect the body. As explained throughout the book, the connection between mind, body and spirit is powerful and remarkable. What we place in our minds will determine whether we follow the good path or stray towards the bad path. Each day is a new beginning and we are faced with choices from the moment we awake. It is ultimately our own choices that drive the life force we are given.

I have explained how learning the higher qualities and employing greater virtues can help sustain us on a spiritual plateau and improve the quality, conduct and power of our lives. Learning the physical disciplines, and then employing the greater virtues raises life to the dignity of an art.

If you can also live up to each of the words that enliven the virtues, understanding their definitions and qualities and apply them not only to yourself but also in your interaction with others, then you have gained the power and can implement the art that living really offers.

If you choose a step, study a point, practice a discipline, employ a virtue, understand the meaning of a righteous word, just one at a time, you're on your way! Add another step, point, discipline, virtue, and word then another only as you feel that you comfortably can. You will eventually improve your overall daily routines and unleash the true power and art of living.

Just take it one day at a time. Review the information and deploy a plan or program of your own. Re-inform, review and then re-deploy. You can accomplish whatever possible after a series of learning experiences, patience and with time. Learning to perfect yourself is the ultimate assignment that can also be the most challenging of all. It improves society and benefits the world in the offing.

If you keep up with current information in the areas of health and fitness, review the active programs for participation and follow the ways explained as they become more comfortable, you will begin to accomplish other goals and objectives and quickly see the improvement in the overall quality of your life. If you choose to follow your truer nature, limits evaporate, time becomes timeless and you will free your mind and soul of pollutants.

If you choose not to follow the righteous path then your mind will affect your body in a negative way. Inner yearnings, hostilities, anger, and fear will give you various health problems like ulcers, heart disease, depression, or other unnecessary physical, emotional and mental maladies.

With great art in the world, great composers and authors, positive energy and spirituality, inspiration and profound insights that great spiritual leaders have given us, we should really not stray from a righteous path. It's very possible, and probable. However, this is if you take the healthy and honest approach toward initiative.

However, if you choose to walk down the easier or evil road, you are taking a shortcut that can lead you away from the right path and into a void. You are also polluting yourself along the way and the result is unimaginable.

Pollutants to the human spirit include: greed, envy, jealousy, false perfectionism, stress, anger, selfishness, materialism, corruption, abuse, crime, and any other kinds of self-destructive and anti-social behavior.

Inaction and amorality are eventually as bad as bad action and immorality. It all catches up with you. Desperation in life, desire for money, unnecessary physical weaknesses, and mental deficiencies which are all usually correctable can also precipitate more evil. Unhealthy behavior or a poor support system can spring from a bad or dysfunctional upbringing, environment, evil company or friends, and other circumstances. However, the warning signs are always there. You need to be honest with yourself and decide that life with true happiness is really more important to you and those surrounding you.

I honestly believe that to become a more compassionate, humble and loving person, you need to go through a number of spiritual tests along the way. However, these can make you stronger, better aware and able to see clearly through the imperfections.

Sometimes you can't attain wisdom or have insight or intuition unless you suffer, or feel the pain or have a tragedy in life. This is unfortunate. You must strive for what you believe in no matter what the prevailing circumstances are.

Some people seem to develop wisdom or insight, have intuition or become enlightened quite readily. Others can't get there because they are spiritually blocked, lack the patience that is necessary for change or have internal or external conflicts that don't allow them to recognize the truth. Everyone goes through sets of problems, either financial, illness or other traumas. Some people choose to wallow in it all. Others strive to develop their spiritual connection by working and developing new insights, by breaking bad habits and replacing them with good ones.

It's great to recover from something negative and rise to a new life filled with joy, happiness, love, peace, freedom, and trust. We all make mistakes in our lives but we all don't learn from them. Learning from mistakes brings you one step closer to that spiritual plateau.

There are always higher purposes presenting themselves to you in life even if you don't always recognize or wonder what those purposes might be. The design of each correct purpose is to make you a better human being, alive with values in a spiritual image. It's about living better, giving back to people and otherwise helping others.

You have to see life as a miracle and believe that miracles can and will happen if you allow yourself to be open to them. Life is a challenge with many rewards as we learn, grow, talk, relate, and listen. Many of life's purposes transcend human understanding. However, much of what we learn in life we will better understand if we apply ourselves to learning, evolve and eventually allow better attitudes and attributes to enrich us.

Do you want to become a better person? Then learn to be more compassionate and kind in your relationships. Kindness comes back, if not from a particular experience, perhaps in another way entirely but that way will help you grow.

Striving toward self-perfection is a constant struggle. Getting beyond prejudice and becoming more tolerant, learning to be less judgmental and open to positive events and energy as they enrich your life isn't easy. Yet, in a simple way, becoming a better person is both natural and human. Trying to control, dominate or manipulate others is not and never will be a path leading to anything but destruction.

Another way to develop character is to live your life with your own correct vision. Get rid of those other negative feelings and become more secure. What you already have in mind might be just what the doctor would have ordered. However, you should never put someone else down or make fun of others even because they're wrong because it can all come back to haunt you. It's also a sure sign of your own inability to be able to properly cope with yourself or others in general.

If you have an agenda that is totally self-motivated, for your own interest and if you become absorbed in that agenda, you need to desist. You must find something more altruistic to support your vision because you can't support yourself while simultaneously ignoring or misusing others. It's just not going to happen that way.

Since happiness comes from within, you can't constantly try to please everyone else. You can't really help everyone, especially if they don't want to be helped. Be careful and choose wisely who you feel that you need to please.

I've learned much from training over the years with many great martial art masters that I felt were well-chosen for their abilities. One particular teacher, Master Richard Kim, conducted karate camp in Southern California. I'll always remember the experience.

We would wake up at five-thirty in the morning and go outside and practice tai chi, paqua and kung fu. He would talk about the spiritual aspects of the arts and discuss the power of the word dignity. How you can become an excellent person.

I'll always remember his profound discussions about the lessons of life and the meaning of the moves that we practice. How each movement is like art and how the movements affect the importance of your life.

We would break for lunch and he would speak about Chinese, American and German history. His discussions were about the nature of reality in comparison to physics, great art, music, and the order of the universe as represented by great playwrights and authors. He was like an encyclopedia of knowledge and truly multifaceted. He has been referred to by many in the field as a truly classical man and artist of life.

Master Kim would have us practice Oriental weapons like the six foot bo-tonfa, sai, kamas, or nunchaku. He explained the focus and exercise connected with these practices and improvement of hand-eye coordination with the alertness that each weapon brings to mind.

We would also practice kata, the formal exercise of karate. He explained the hidden aspects of each move and the forces and dynamics of the proper way of positioning and moving your body.

He also pointed out that, "Kata is the soul of the martial arts." He taught the students the value and morality of the martial arts that far exceed other physical techniques. He emphasized spirituality in all of his conversations and developed a high level of knowledge in other fields and areas outside of the martial arts, bringing that knowledge to all of his classes.

He would teach us about meditation and the science and technique of sparring. He was well-versed in philosophy and whenever he told a story you would remember it because he related each story to how it could affect your own life.

Another great Sensei that I remember well is Sensei Peter Urban. He thoroughly enjoyed the philosophy and psychology of the martial arts. He always said in class, "Today is now." You have to live your life today as if it were your last day because one doesn't know about tomorrow. He always left me with a bit of inspiration and discipline.

I would ask him how he was doing and he would reply, "Better than ever." I always thought that it was an interesting way of answering because it's good to keep a positive attitude. He believed that commitment to the art or whatever you believe in can get you through anything.

I know that commitment can solidify your relationships and bring friends closer to you. It is also part of the learning process that includes others and an important step in the direction of accomplishment.

What I have discovered through each of these martial art experiences is that if practiced with enthusiasm, martial arts will jumpstart your ability to learn, increase the opportunity to appreciate selflessness and better position you to live the higher virtues. It will give you a better perception and awareness of yourself and surroundings and make you cognizant of understanding people behind the masks or facades that they present. You will quickly see through to the inner qualities another person does or doesn't possess.

As a child, young adult or adult you can always begin to apply the right concepts of physical fitness, good health and discipline, including the martial arts, to living your daily life and routines. Each day is a new beginning. Just take it one step at a time and as you do, you will unleash the true power and art of living.

# Conclusion

A conclusion usually means an ending. This book has no real conclusion or ending. The ending should become the beginning or continuation of your physical, mental and spiritual development. And, there is no end to the spiritual, which is perfection of the total person, including the physical and mental aspects of a being. It all includes learning and deploying the higher qualities, living on a spiritual plateau and then taking what we have learned in the spiritual world back into the real world and with us into the world hereafter.

I have envisioned a perfect utopian society which of course thus far in the world does not exist. Nonetheless, in our minds it can and together we can strive to make it happen. Some of the great thinkers and philosophers of the past: Socrates, Plato, Sir Thomas Moore, Mahatma Gandhi, Abraham Lincoln and many others certainly envisioned improved societies to which many have and continue to aspire.

There should also be courses in formal secular education better defining moral values as well as teaching students how to turn theory into practice. Too often one completes a course of study with little or no practical purpose because there has been no transitional lesson taught as to value application.

Even in life, how often do we truly learn from experience, either our own or from others? Altruism, idealism, pragmatism, and so many more concepts that haven't been elaborated upon in this book are certainly ways of life worthy of aspiration. Anything that can bring positive energy to the spirit is of benefit in relation to the rest of our lives.

Our mission on earth also includes assisting other people. It is wise to be true to one's self in order to better help our neighbor. I believe that understanding the mind, body and spirit connection is truly appreciating the need for proper physical, emotional and mental wellbeing as well as living life on a right spiritual plateau. Employing the greater virtues in life and seeking new higher qualities to aspire toward should never end. The quest is filled with brave and bountiful new beginnings.

Many of the great masters have believed that the source of much of this knowledge is already within us and that humankind already has the answers that it needs. There must be a way to get closer to the innate talents and somewhat inanimate answers that can support our daily experiences and foster further growth. We have to be able to redefine life and experience reality to its fullest with joy.

If you have ever been inspired, enlightened, strengthened, or have attained wisdom in your life, then meditate on those experiences, reflect on their sources, pray, and be grateful. Eventually, the totality of life in all its reality including all its understanding and mystery will begin to shine forth. Life is so very special and the joy that can come not only to us but also through us for the benefit of others is unbounded.

Life is truly a miracle. Singularly as well as together we can indeed create miracles.